5.50

ur vacation
at 1976
July
A.D.

OUR LIVING WORLD OF NATURE

The
Life
of Prairies
and Plains

Developed jointly with The World Book Encyclopedia

Produced with the cooperation of
The United States Department of the Interior

OUR LIVING WORLD OF NATURE

The Life of Prairies and Plains

DURWARD L. ALLEN

Published in cooperation with
The World Book Encyclopedia
McGraw-Hill Book Company
NEW YORK   TORONTO   LONDON

DURWARD L. ALLEN *is a native of Fort Wayne, Indiana, where his interest in nature and the out-of-doors developed at an early age. He received a degree in zoology from the University of Michigan and a Ph.D. degree in vertebrate ecology from Michigan State College. As a research biologist for ten years with the Michigan Game Division, he developed two wildlife experiment stations and carried out studies on the fox squirrel, pheasant, cottontail rabbit, skunk, and other wildlife. After military service in World War II he spent an additional eight years with the U.S. Fish and Wildlife Service in Maryland and Washington, D.C. Leaving a position as Assistant Chief, Branch of Wildlife Research, he joined the staff of Purdue University, Lafayette, Indiana, where he is Professor of Wildlife Ecology in the Department of Forestry and Conservation. Recent investigations by Dr. Allen and his students have been oriented toward problems of predator-prey relationships, big-game management, and wilderness preservation, featuring such species as deer, moose, beaver, wolf, and coyote. Dr. Allen is a past president of the Wildlife Society and the recipient of several national awards for his books, scientific papers, and magazine articles in the field of wildlife biology and conservation.*

Library of Congress Catalog Card Number: 67–15849

7890 NR 72

ISBN 07-001099-4

OUR LIVING WORLD OF NATURE

Contents

MEN OF YESTERDAY 169

APPENDIX

Empire
of the Sun

Grass . . . It clothes the bareness of land and heals raw wounds against the wind. It softens the beat of rain and soaks water gently into its mellow ground. A century ago a Kansas senator, John J. Ingalls, called grass "the forgiveness of Nature—her constant benediction." IIe had a feeling for the earth and saw its need.

Of our planet's total land surface, about a quarter was at one time covered with grass. This is the characteristic vegetation of areas having dry subsoil and seasonal moisture in the upper layers. Such lands receive less rainfall than forested country and are more exposed to drying winds. Famous grasslands of the earth are the steppes of Eurasia, the African veldt, the North American prairies and plains, and the Argentine pampas.

Among the earth's habitats important to man, grassland probably has been more misused than any other. In extensive regions, moving desert sands have taken over where protecting swards once secured the soil. Man has not managed the land well in semiarid climates.

In truth, we should look hard at the life communities of grasslands. Through millions of years these combinations of plants and animals assembled and organized themselves.

They found a way to survive, reproduce, and store a surplus of life-sustaining substance in the soil. This they did in environments harshened by extremes of temperature, aridity, and violent winds.

In North America our great central grassland is disappearing. Few samples of the original vegetation are left. Nowhere do we have the primitive plant-animal community as it was in early times. Some of its important creatures have died out completely.

Scientists would give much to see that region of far horizons as it was in the early days of exploration by the white man. So would a host of other people who delight in the out-of-doors. Nothing on earth was quite like this tawny-carpeted wilderness with its millions of bison and antelope, its patrolling wolves, its burrowing hordes, its spectacular waves of feathered migrants, its air vibrant with the cry of curlews and the trumpeting of cranes.

Let us visit that primitive scene and piece together from historical records and modern studies the story of the original grassland on our own continent. Then, leapfrogging through space and time, we shall bring that story up to the present. We shall begin by turning back the clock of centuries to the year 1491 and then board some imaginary flying craft, highly maneuverable and silent-running, soaring over the beaches of New England. It was not New England then, but we shall use today's names for places and things because it is the easy way.

Of course, 1491 is the year before an adventurous Italian named Christopher Columbus, flying the Spanish flag, made a landfall with his three cranky little vessels on an island in the Caribbean. We shall see North America before the white man began his endless overhauling of the land.

Outliers in the East

It is early spring on the New England coast. A northwest wind bears the chill of snowfields that still clog shaded forests between here and Hudson Bay. Sandy barrens spread out below us. These are largely covered by heath-type

A great flock of snow geese, perhaps tens of thousands strong, swings over the North Dakota prairie, a stopover point on its migration route between the Gulf Coast and the breeding grounds north of Hudson Bay.

10

Before the white man's arrival, the heath hen, the easternmost of the prairie chickens, flourished along the Middle Atlantic Coast in country like this: sandy, windswept clearings of grasses and low-growing shrubs set in sparse forests of scrub oak and pitch pine. Today, this habitat has given way to America's densest concentration of cities and industries, and the heath hen is gone forever.

shrubs and bordered by scrub oaks. We hear something, a throbbing, cooing noise that seems to come from all around us.

There they are on a grassy knoll, half a hundred bantam-sized birds cross-barred in tan and buff, the strutting males with bright inflated sacs like an orange on each side of the neck. This is a *booming ground* of the heath hen. Something exciting to watch at close range is happening here.

The males are spaced out over a couple of acres. Each is guarding a small *territory*, an area bounded by imaginary lines that no other male may cross. Where two territories meet, the cocks frequently clash breast to breast in a picking, wing-beating fight. Then the question of property lines is settled, and they retreat and strut again, spreading their tails, dragging wings, pattering feet, inflating air sacs, and uttering their *coo-hoo-oo* booming call.

Females wander unconcerned over the booming area from one territory to another. One might think they just happened to be there. But sooner or later each will accept a male and mating will take place. Then the hens will scatter to their nesting places.

If we were to wander widely over these coastal lands, we would find the heath cocks dancing from Virginia to Maine. Theirs is a ritualized mating display such as is seen among grassland grouse the world over.

Grassland? Yes, these are displaced prairie chickens, though of course they are now well adapted to the sandy coastal barrens. This change must have come about after the population was cut off and isolated from other prairie chickens inhabiting the prairies and plains farther west. After the ice age a great dry spell held out for more than a thousand years, bringing about an eastward extension of our central grassland. Then the climate turned moist again, and forests closed in on the openings. Trees reoccupied most of the country south of the Great Lakes. Possibly that is how these chickens were stranded in the East.

This is but one episode in the history of our continent since the great ice sheet of the last glaciation melted back to the north. Geologically, it was yesterday. There was glacial ice hanging on in upper Lake Michigan and in Lake Superior only nine thousand years ago.

Forests on these coastal sands are mostly pitch pine and scrub oak. In September the smoke of fires is common in this region. The dry sites burn readily, and so trees are prevented

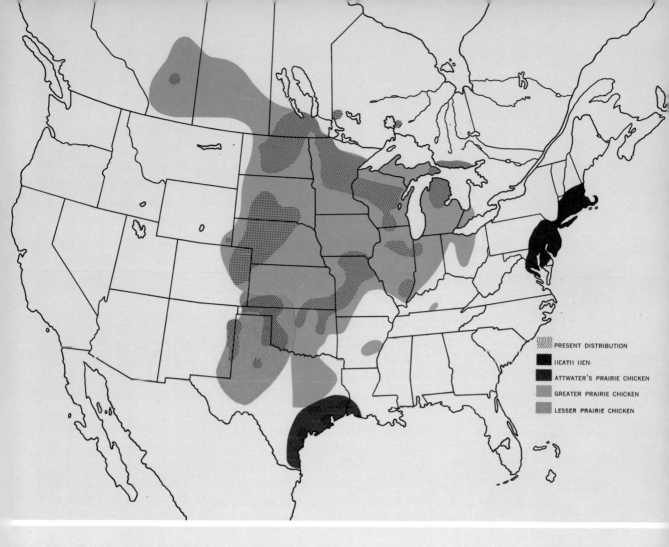

PRESENT DISTRIBUTION
HEATH HEN
ATTWATER'S PRAIRIE CHICKEN
GREATER PRAIRIE CHICKEN
LESSER PRAIRIE CHICKEN

THE VANISHING PRAIRIE CHICKENS

America's four principal subspecies of prairie chickens have not fared well in the four and a half centuries since the landing of Columbus. (Their former distributions are indicated by the color areas on the map.) Even the widely distributed greater prairie chicken is now classified by the Department of the Interior as "rare and decreasing" over much of its range. The lesser prairie chicken has teetered on the brink of extinction since the 1930s; the total number of remaining birds fluctuates from year to year, sometimes running as low as two to three thousand, sometimes reaching about ten thousand. Attwater's prairie chicken, never widely distributed, is so perilously close to extinction that the Department of the Interior has placed it on the "endangered" list. A 1963 census put the population at about thirteen hundred birds, scattered in isolated colonies of a few hundred individuals each along the Gulf Coast of Texas. The fourth subspecies, the heath hen (*right*), is beyond help, despite conscientious (but belated) human efforts to keep the bird from passing into the oblivion of extinction. The last reported sighting of a heath hen was on March 11, 1932.

from overspreading the brushy heaths. It is fire that preserves the openings and the chickens. Farther inland on better soil the more humid forest seldom burns.

In a couple of centuries the European settlers of this region will find it easy to shoot heath hens for their game markets. The pressure will be too much, and the birds will decline rapidly in the nineteenth century. The last known bird of this species will be seen on an island off Cape Cod in the early 1930s, the lone survivor of a species doomed to extinction.

Westward ho!

The bur oak, also known as mossy-cup oak, is a common tree along the border where forest and grassland meet. Reaching heights up to 170 feet, it is the tallest of our more than two dozen species of oaks, although it seldom attains its full height in the prairie-edge country. The big acorns are partially encased in a distinctively fringed burlike "cup," giving the tree both its common names.

We fly on rapidly over a region of orderly ridges still in the winter brown of oak and chestnut. Now to the north we see a broad body of water—Lake Erie—and below us the forest type changes. Columned hard maples and the gray trunks of beeches cover rolling hills. In the distance we see an opening in the forest cover. It is a patch of prairie, a relic of the more extensive grasslands of earlier times. This small prairie has low-lying wet spots, where there are stands of cattail and bur reed bordered by broad meadows of sedge and last year's dry cordgrass. Surrounding the grassland is an oak and hickory forest. On the sunny edges of this grassland there are oaks of a particular kind, with coarse twigs and the broad round tops of trees grown in the open. They are bur oaks, and we shall find them commonly on prairie margins.

Westward we see other prairie openings, and now we are skirting a great swamp that lies across the corner of Ohio. Then on we go over lands, in northern Indiana, dotted with many lakes. This area was a dumping ground for gravelly debris carried by the great glaciers of the ice age. The drier sites are occupied by forests of oak and hickory, which give way again to beech and maple wherever soils are heavier or more moist.

Ahead the scenery changes. A vast marsh extends far to the west. Through its wide expanse below us a slow stream, the Kankakee, winds and wanders in a confusion of loops and oxbows. On its edges, the marsh is extended by ponds and wet meadows behind beaver dams overgrown with brush on tributary streams. The broad wetland is aswarm with migrating ducks and geese. This is the world-famous

Kankakee wildfowling ground. It will be dredged and drained in the early 1900s, and the black soil will become cropland.

On our right a huge body of water extends to the far horizon. Indians of the region call it Michigamea—or something like that, depending on variations in language. North from the Kankakee lowland, and east of the big lake, tongues and islands of dry grassland extend into forested country that will be the corner counties of the state of Michigan. Hemming these prairies are the bur oaks again, large rounded trees growing well spaced in grassy meadows. Some of the parklike stands are completely surrounded by woodland. The pioneers, yet to come, will call them "oak openings."

Flying low over the marsh, we see great activity among the waterfowl. The ducks are in their brightest breeding plumages, and there is a riot of splashing, chasing, courting, displaying, and fighting. Pairing takes place along the migration route, as lengthening hours of daylight activate winter-dormant sex glands and trigger the chain reaction of breeding physiology. Most of these ducks and geese will move on to northern nesting grounds.

Ahead a dense flock of birds rises from the cattails, and we move up to check on the disturbance. There we see them, strung out on the river, six dugout canoes headed downstream on the Kankakee. Tomorrow the Indians will come to a major waterway flowing to the south. Possibly their village is located there. We cannot be certain of this, but in time that big river and a tribe that lives on it will be called Illinois.

Extending far south of us, continuous with the Kankakee marsh, are the Indiana prairies. And scattered here and there are herds of dark-colored grazing animals. From a distance they look like cattle, and indeed they belong to the same family. They are American bison, or buffalo, as frontiersmen in time to come will call them. These will be a familiar sight on our tour of grass country to the west.

Mostly the buffalo are in bands of fifty to two hundred. Inspecting some of them at close range, we see that their shaggy coats are brown, sun-bleached to gold on the hump. Spring shedding has just begun. Here and there a cow is accompanied by a wobbly yellowish-red calf, for in April a few are already born.

We hear prairie chickens booming. One of their dancing grounds is on a sandy island that rises out of the marsh and

The bur oak is the dominant tree of the oak openings. Pleasant, parklike stands of these trees once edged the grasslands through much of the Middle West. The tree is better equipped than many of its relatives to compete with the grasses: its heavy bark, one to two inches thick, provides effective insulation against the fires that periodically sweep through grasslands. Thus, the bur oak often leads the advance wherever the forest encroaches on the grasslands.

Throat sacs puffed out, neck and tail feathers raised, and wings trailing, a male greater prairie chicken executes a stately springtime courtship dance to the accompaniment of his own hollow, booming call. His mate will lay a clutch of ten to fourteen eggs in a nest in the grass, and the young will hatch out after twenty-three days of incubation.

an adjacent wet prairie. The birds look like heath hens, but they are a different race. Biologists of the future will call this bird the greater prairie chicken.

Westward these chickens are dancing over a vast extent of prairies now abloom with spring flowers—dogtooth violet, anemone, buttercup, and pasqueflower. Coming on rapidly to ornament the grassland are yellow star grass, wild onion, vetch, and many more.

The buffalo are mainly on greener parts of the range, and a close look tells us why. Last fall a fire swept through here, taking off the heavy growth of dry grasses as well as an area of sedges and cattails in the adjacent marsh. In late winter the blackened ash and stubble absorbed the sun's rays and warmed the ground, contributing to the rapid melting of snow and an early green-up. Now this land furnishes the best available pasturage. One group of settlers in Illinois grasslands to the west will name their town Greenup.

As we move southward along the prairie margins, bur oaks

are a familiar sight. It is evident that last year's ground fire burned among the trees without harming them, for this kind of oak has a thick fire-resistant bark. There is no clue to how these stands got their start; but they obviously can grow in prairie edges where other woody plants cannot. Conditions are different along the streams, for these moist sites are thick with a variety of shrubs and trees. The dark lines of watercourses, just taking on the green of spring, are clearly marked on the open lands before us.

At the edge of the grasslands

Time has gone by, and it is now June. We are still in the land of prairie borders, and we soar high for a better view. Slanting rays of the afternoon sun bring out in sharp relief the modeling of the land surface and the pattern of woodland and grass for hundreds of miles westward.

Scattered bison, including a number of youngsters like the two in the foreground, graze placidly in lush spring grass spangled with bright flowers. The calves, a product of the previous summer's breeding season, are born from April through June. By autumn, their reddish-yellow wool will be replaced by the dark, shaggy coat of the adults.

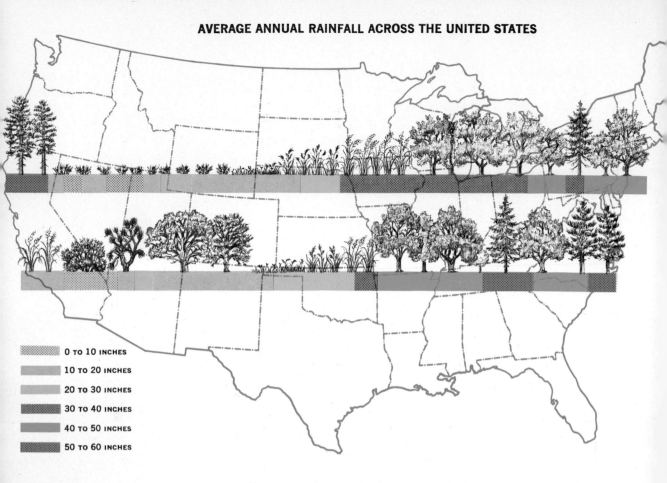

0 TO 10 INCHES
10 TO 20 INCHES
20 TO 30 INCHES
30 TO 40 INCHES
40 TO 50 INCHES
50 TO 60 INCHES

This map shows the average annual rainfall and typical vegetation of the United States at two latitudes. The mosaic of plant communities spread across America's face is the product of soil chemistry, temperature, length of growing season, prevailing wind patterns, and, above all, amount of rainfall. The superabundance of rain in the Northwest gives rise to lush rain forests; the lack of rain in the Southwest reduces vegetation there to the tough, highly specialized plants of the desert. In areas of moderate rainfall, the grasses and the forests struggle for dominance.

Over most of this region of Illinois and Iowa, large and small grasslands are mixed with areas of forest. Here we have an eastward extension of prairies that are largely unbroken west of the Missouri River. Obviously, this is a zone of competition between the broad-leaved forests, mostly oak and hickory in the uplands, and the open country featuring grasses of tall and medium heights. Stretches of forest and grass alternate, according to local conditions, all the way across to the Nebraska line. Where trees will grow and where grasses will grow is decided by a combination of seasonal rainfall, temperature, and the surface features of the land.

Even a quick look at the *biomes*, or major life regions, of North America indicates that temperature, humidity, and other climatic conditions play an important part in determining vegetation types: that is, whether we shall have a desert (very dry climate), a grassland (semiarid), or a forest (humid to wet). Here on the forest edges annual rainfall totals thirty-five inches. Westward in eastern Nebraska the amount declines to twenty-five inches. Winter is the drier season.

This region supports woodland on many sites, but extensive well-drained lowlands and more level uplands are in tallgrass. Regular burning does not harm the grasses, but it kills the sprouts and seedlings of trees and shrubs which could otherwise take these areas over. Thus, the tallgrass prairie is a grassland in a forest climate, maintained by fire.

As we travel widely across northern Illinois into Iowa and Missouri, these relationships become more evident. Trees follow the drainageways, but on the eastern edges of lakes and rivers more extensive woodlands are common. Since winds are mainly from the west, the water has acted as a firebreak. Trees persist also on steep slopes and rocky ridges, since grasses do not grow lush enough to carry a hot fire.

The prairie-edge region is the home of certain wildlife species that do well in a mixed cover of trees, shrubs, and grasses. On bright mornings male bobwhites are calling from streamhead thickets or upland clumps of hazel, wild plum, and sassafras. In deep sods along these coverts cottontail rabbits are nesting. Fox squirrels have long since given birth to their first litters in hollow tree trunks or bulky leaf nests high in the treetops.

Cottontails thrive in prairie-edge habitats everywhere. The doe brings forth as many as five litters of four to seven blind, hairless young each year. The nest is a pocket in the sod, lined with dry grass and tufts of the doe's fur. Within two weeks the young are venturing from the nest. Some will breed in the summer of their birth, but most will bear their first litters the following spring.

A male indigo bunting—his mate is a plain drab brown— delivers a caterpillar to a nest of hungry youngsters. This handsome little bird, about the size of an English sparrow, nests in brushy tangles bordering open grassland, generally only a few feet above the ground. The male usually sings from a high perch and is often heard during the heat of a summer day when most of his neighbors are silent.

These are creatures with a future. In the post-Indian era, forests of the Great Lakes region will be largely cleared for farms. Then the bobwhite, rabbit, and fox squirrel will move into these artificial prairie edges, far beyond their present range. They will be "farm game," capable of thriving wherever a good balance is maintained between crop fields, brushy cover, and woods.

Birds of this region show adaptations that differ strikingly between forest and prairie. Along woodland edges singing male indigo buntings are spaced out on their territories. In brushy edges cardinals, catbirds, brown thrashers, prairie warblers, and song sparrows have divided up available habitats in similar fashion.

These birds of the brush and woodland edges habitually sing from perches. In the prairie some species, such as the dickcissel, the meadowlark, and certain sparrows, may sing from the swaying stem of a tall flower stalk. In marshes the red-winged blackbirds commonly do this. But many grass-

land species sing in flight—longspurs of several kinds, pipits, horned larks, and the bobolink, lark bunting, and upland plover. Needless to say, these are ground nesters, true creatures of the grass.

The season is advancing, and we must get along. Traveling north and west from central Iowa, we find tallgrass prairies nearly continuous. The forests are left to the south. From here on, well across the Canadian border, this lush range is broken only by lakes, sloughs, streams, and the wooded flood plain of a great river the red man calls "Father of Waters," the mighty Mississippi.

The eastern margins of this prairie land are marked by bur oaks. And beyond these edges the forest has a familiar look. Here is the same hard maple we saw in Ohio, but there is no beech. Its place is taken by basswood, which has a tough inner bark used by Indians for woven mats and for other purposes.

Nearly everywhere the open land is a network of trails,

This meadowlark, about the size of a robin, nests on the ground, protected by tall, overhanging grasses and its own camouflage color pattern. A characteristic inhabitant of the grasslands, the meadowlark spends most of its time on the ground, flicking its tail as it walks along in search of insects and seeds. It takes to the air only to avoid an intruder or to reach a low perch from which it delivers its pleasant song.

21

and bison herds are a common sight as we move rapidly over the freshly green countryside. We notice that often the old bulls are in small groups keeping largely to themselves. May and early June is the period of calf drop, and now rusty red youngsters are seen in all the cow bands. Scouting such herds are the large plains wolves, some of so light a shade that they appear pure white in the distance. This strikingly beautiful race of wolf will be extinct before the end of the nineteenth century.

Flying westward over the Minnesota–South Dakota border, we find the land pitted and pocked with thousands of small marshes. This is to become famous as the prairie pothole country. It stretches northwest into the grasslands of

Canada and is the most important nesting ground for ducks in North America. Great flights of waterfowl move in with the spring. Many of them courted and paired on temporary waters in wet grasslands farther south.

The pothole ponds are ringed with cattails, bulrushes, reeds, and whitetop grass. Such diving ducks as the canvasback, redhead, and ruddy are making their nests on mounds of plant debris over the water. The potholes are likewise the rearing place for broods of dabbling ducks such as the mallard, teal, and pintail, which are hatched in nearby uplands.

Now we must turn south again and make many stops over this region of the prairie. Knowing its outlines, let us take a closer look from ground level.

Countless thousands of pothole ponds and marshes were left by the glaciers over a broad belt of the northern grasslands. These wetlands are nesting sites for great numbers of ducks and marsh birds. Many potholes have been drained by man, with a resultant decline in our waterfowl populations.

Land of the tallgrasses

Here and there, where streams have undercut their banks, we can see the layered structure of the soil. If we compare the soil profiles of an area of broad-leaved forest and an area of tallgrass, some differences are evident.

Under the surface litter of the forest floor, there are a few inches of dark topsoil, below which the subsoil is light in color and sparsely penetrated by tree roots. Eventually these roots will die and leave small amounts of organic matter in lower levels.

In contrast, the tallgrass prairie has a dark, humus-rich topsoil commonly from one to two feet deep. It is a mass of fibrous roots. Wherever moisture conditions permit, the tallgrasses flourish and spread by underground stems, forming dense sods. If we were to stake out an acre in one of these thick stands of western Iowa, skim off a surface layer four inches thick, and then wash out all the soil, we would leave a great spongy pile of grass roots weighing four and a half tons! The prairie sod is so tough that white settlers will need five yoke of oxen to pull the breaking plow.

In forested areas, the subsoil is moist all the way down to the zone of underground water. Commonly this is true under the tallgrass prairie too. But there even the subsoil is darkened by humus left when the copious roots of grasses and other herbs died and decomposed. The roots of these prairie grasses grow downward twelve feet or more. They absorb water from all levels and with it bring up minerals to the growing plant. An abundance of dead vegetation is deposited on the surface, and at the end of each growing season it will rot and become available as nutrients for new generations of plants.

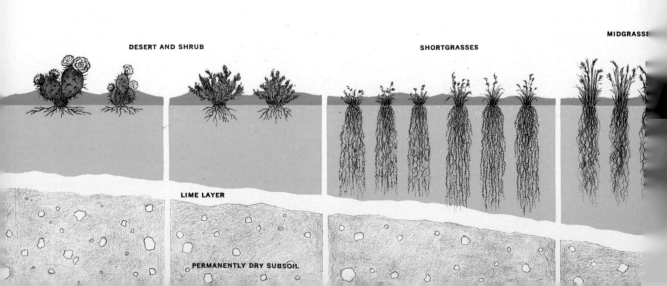

DESERT AND SHRUB   SHORTGRASSES   MIDGRASSE

LIME LAYER

PERMANENTLY DRY SUBSOIL

The soil of the tallgrass prairie varies from slightly acid to slightly alkaline. Deep and mellow, it is a storehouse of fertility built up over long periods of time. This is the most productive agricultural land on earth, and this region will some day be the "corn belt," where a Central American grass called maize will become one of man's foremost crops.

Grasses are deep and rank on broad stretches of flood plain and other level ground, which commonly are wet for several weeks in spring. Over thousands of acres, tall blue-stem, six to eight feet high, waves and rustles in the wind. With it are the equally tall Indian grass; airy stands of switch grass, with its finely dispersed tops; and in low places, where it is wetter, dense masses of slough grass. With these there frequently is an intermixture of Canada wild rye, with its distinctive nodding heads.

These are the grasses of which it will be told that they were high enough to be tied together over the back of a horse. It is their dense, well-cured tinder that, in fall or spring, carries fire over this land at almost the speed of wind. The prairie is burned every year near the bark-covered lodges of Indian villages in streamside groves, for the red men have learned that the buffalo can be hunted handily when they come in to the burns for early grazing. Sometimes natural fires are started by the lightning associated with "dry" storms. If we fly at night above one of these burned areas, we see thousands of pinpoints of light scattered over the land. They are glowing "buffalo chips"—the dried droppings of buffalo—that smolder for hours in the wake of a fire. Under the right conditions a new wind may carry their sparks far ahead to light more fires on the prairie. We might say that, in a sense, the buffalo helps to burn and improve his own pasturage.

The soil beneath the grasslands is characterized by a rich black humus formed from the decomposition of countless grass roots. Below the tallgrasses, this layer of humus reaches depths of twelve feet. Below the midgrasses and shortgrasses, it reaches down to the lime layer, the stratum of light-colored soil rich in carbonates and other minerals which marks the level to which rain water penetrates, and below which the subsoil is permanently dry. No lime layer exists beneath the forest and the tallgrasses, since the rain water here reaches all the way down to subsoil kept permanently moist by underground water.

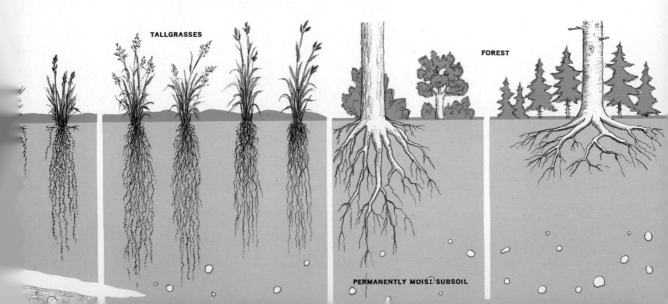

TALLGRASSES

FOREST

PERMANENTLY MOIST SUBSOIL

THE TALLGRASSES

The tallgrasses flourished on the
eastern prairies where rainfall is
relatively heavy; they could also
be found in the moist lowlands and
deep ravines of more westerly
plains country. Tall bluestem
(*left*), sometimes soaring eight feet
above the ground and thrusting
roots six feet into the prairie soil,
formed dense stands through
which spring and autumn prairie
fires raced with awesome speed.
Switch grass (*center*), about a
foot shorter than tall bluestem,
requires less moisture than
bluestem and so thrived on the
warmer and drier sites of the
tallgrass prairie. Indian grass
(*right*) is similar to tall bluestem
in height and in its rainfall
requirements and, though far less
abundant, was found mixed with
bluestem throughout its range.

26

The midgrasses

Far and wide over the prairie we have noticed that grasses of the drier uplands are not so tall. Commonly they grow two to four feet in height and are classified as midgrasses. For the most part they grow in bunches or clumps, rather than in sods. From Indiana to western Iowa and Missouri, the midgrasses increase their coverage, far exceeding tallgrasses in the western half of this range.

The most abundant and important midgrass is little bluestem. Like the tallgrasses, except wild rye, and other kinds of bluestem we shall see, this one originated somewhere in a warm climate to the south. Thus, it makes its best growth through the hot part of summer. In the eastern fringes of the prairie, little bluestem occupies the driest upland sites. Far to the west, on the apron of the Rocky Mountains, it may still be seen, this time on the more moist situations in arid shortgrass country. From north to south it ranges from Canada to the Texas coast. Two other warm-season midgrasses of this range are prairie dropseed and side-oats grama. Several species closely related to these will be common in drier ranges even farther west.

Other abundant midgrasses are needlegrass and June grass. These and several low sedges become the dominant plants on large areas to the north. They originated in a cool climate, and so it is not surprising that they make their growth in the cool season early in the year, and again in late fall. This mixture of warm-season and cool-season grasses helps to ensure the productivity of prairies, regardless of when the rains come in any particular year.

In early June the yellowing stems of needlegrass are weighted with fruits. The swaying stand bows in a deep wave as a gust of wind passes over the uplands. Pick some of the slender pointed fruits, or seeds, and look at them closely. Each has a five-inch twisted "beard," or *awn*, projecting from its tip. After the seed is shed, the first moisture causes the

The distinctive flowering stalk of side-oats grama (*above*) is arranged so that its drooping, seed-bearing spikes all extend to one side of the central axis. Needle and thread (*below*) gets its name from the sharp-pointed seed (the "needle") and its long, twisted awn (the "thread"). Both these plants are typical of the warm midgrass prairie.

28

Split-beard bluestem is easily identified by its distinctive paired seed heads topping its slender two- to four-foot stems. This species is considered one of the less desirable of the midgrasses, being too "stemmy" to provide good forage for grazing animals. It is an invader species that often dominates overgrazed or otherwise abused ranges.

awn to straighten. Then, in drying out, it twists again and screws the seed into the soil, where it can germinate. Needle and thread, a closely related species that is more common westward, has wavy or curled awns. With the pointed seed they suggest a threaded needle. Needlegrasses are important forage for grazing animals around the world in the Northern Hemisphere. Fossil evidence of such a grass has been found with remains of *Merychippus*, a three-toed horse that grazed the North American grasslands in the Miocene epoch, some twenty million years ago.

Growing abundantly with the needlegrass in northern prairies is western wheatgrass. We quickly learn to recognize its blue-green stands at some distance. It is another cool-season species that spreads by underground stems over areas of bare soil to form loose sods. Western wheatgrass, which is widely distributed and drought-resistant, will have an important future in the white man's grazing industry on northern plains.

29

THE MIDGRASSES

Where rainfall is less abundant, and in the prairie uplands where wind and sun rob the land of much of its moisture, the tallgrasses give way to the midgrasses, species that grow two to four feet high. Most of the midgrasses are bunch formers and do not produce deep, root-tangled sods like those of the tallgrasses. Little bluestem (*right*) does form sod wherever it finds sufficient moisture, but through most of its wide range it is found in clumps like these shown growing with western ragweed. Western wheatgrass (*center*) is a hardy, drought-resistant species that often takes over disturbed sites and large expanses where prolonged dryness kills off other grasses. June grass (*left*) is native to the cooler northern prairies, where it is found mixed with the more dominant little bluestem and needlegrasses.

Flowering herbs and shrubs

In each of the differing prairie habitats, we find deep-rooted flowering herbs, those broad-leaved nongrassy species that will be called *forbs* by range men, and just "weeds" by gardeners. They help to vary and brighten, through spring and summer, the swards of growing greens and ripening yellows and browns. Colorful forbs will spangle the open lands with successive bloomings until at last the October frosts close the growing season. Scattered over the range is every hue of yellow, purple, blue, pink, brown, and white. Each in its proper time and situation, we find blazing star, coneflower, prairie clover, wallflower, wild indigo, bergamot, red mallow, vervain, leadplant, brown-eyed Susan, fleabane, boneset, ironweed, and a dazzling array of sunflowers, asters, and goldenrods. Indians know well the edible roots of this flora, especially *Psoralea*, or prairie turnip, and a streamside sunflower that will be called Jerusalem artichoke.

In moist depressions the stands of slough grass, switch grass, nodding wild rye, and scouring rush are intermixed with broad-leaved weeds: some of the commonest are blue flag, water hemlock, meadow rue, smartweed, phlox, and swamp milkweed. Especially noticeable in these situations are several kinds of rosinweed, including prairie dock, cup plant, and compass plant, all bearing tall late-summer stalks of yellow flowers.

One conceives of prairies and plains as covered with grasses and other herbs—and so they are. But, particularly in the

The compass plant, a forb of the tallgrass regions, sometimes reaches a height of ten feet. Its leaves tend to align themselves in a north-south plane, giving the plant its common name.

A fritillary butterfly perches atop a purple coneflower (*left*) with drooping petallike rays surrounding a central cluster of tiny true flowers. This forb of the midgrass prairies blooms in early summer; the rays drop off after about a month, while the flower clusters last until late fall. The little prairie rose (*right*), a true woody shrub, graces the uplands with pink and white flowers in June and shining red fruits from July through the autumn.

This purple prairie clover and native bumble bee are a good example of the interdependence of the plants and animals of the prairie community. The clover provides the bumble bee with food in the form of pollen and nectar; the bumble bee helps propagate the clover by spreading pollen from one plant to another. The prairie clover and other legumes take part in another, less obvious "joint effort": their roots give shelter to special bacteria that enrich the soil by "fixing" nitrogen from the air into mineral salts usable by the clover and other plants.

North, there are low-growing shrubs that obviously have a place in this dry region. The commonest woody plant, seen far and wide, is wolfberry, a kind of snowberry. Acres of it are a common sight in the Dakota pothole country. Often the stands are mixed or interspersed with shining thickets of silverberry that flash a wave of white as wind blows across them, turning their hoary leaves to the sun. Farther west buffalo berry, another silvery shrub, becomes plentiful. And we have grown accustomed to the prickly coverts of Wood's rose. The true prairie rose is smaller and much more widely distributed to the south.

Many of the healthiest stands of shrubs are on steep north-facing slopes. These are slightly cooler situations, not so sun-baked, and they offer slightly better moisture conditions. Here is where we find heavy thickets of chokecherry. A small related species, sand cherry, grows on the open prairie of Nebraska. All these woody plants are spread by fruit-eating birds and mammals. The pits are stored and eaten like small nuts by many kinds of rodents. The fires that come with dry periods probably keep the shrubs from becoming more abundant than they are.

As we move about, enjoying the flowers of the prairie, something seems to be missing—and now we know what it is. Where are the honey bees? The answer applies to a great many other living things that will be familiar to Americans of the twentieth century. It will be during the 1600s that honey bees are introduced from Europe and naturalized in North America. Nearly all the common weeds of the Old World will be brought over as seed to take their places in the vegetation of this continent. An inquiring botanist will list 263 kinds of foreign plants among the vegetation of Iowa. About the same number of species make up the primitive prairie flora of the state.

It is characteristic that perennial grasses and other species of the prairie are long-lived. An individual plant may live ten to twenty years and develop a root system with a much larger bulk than that of its aboveground parts.

In exploring this vegetation, we have seen fresh digging here and there. A part of it is done by ground squirrels, but something larger has been at work. Now we have caught up with him. Across that draw is a squat, stubby animal with a heavy pelt of salt-and-pepper gray and short black legs. It must weigh fifteen pounds. It is digging, throwing slugs of soil backward with its hind feet as it bores ahead with its long-clawed forefeet.

It is a badger, largest member of the weasel family in this

The badger's white stripe, extending from its nose over the top of its head and down its back, positively identifies this big member of the weasel family. A tireless burrower, the badger spends much of its time digging out ground squirrels and other small rodents that are the staple of its diet. Badgers are not aggressive, but if provoked these strong, stocky animals will defend themselves with startling ferocity.

Prairie phlox, bearing its five-petaled flowers on stems a foot to two and a half feet tall, brightens the midgrass prairies during May and June. The hairy calyx, the green cuplike part of the flower, gives the plant another common name, downy phlox, as well as its scientific name *Phlox pilosa*.

region of the grass. Come to think of it, badgers will be found in every kind of grass country all the way to the Pacific Coast. This one is digging out a ground squirrel, a job for which it is well equipped with its keen nose, its big appetite, and its earth-mover build. Digging out the burrows of rodents is a good life by badger standards.

Mixed prairie

We have crossed the Missouri River. In eastern Nebraska we reach the limits of the tallgrass prairie. Tall bluestem here is not so tall and is restricted to the lowest ground, where there is more moisture; midgrasses dominate the cover far and wide. Moving on, we must endure the torrid heat of summer. This is a realm of brilliant sun, brassy noonday skies, hot winds, and a high evaporation rate. Here the annual rainfall is only about twenty-three inches, and the character of the soil reflects this.

It is still dark with abundant humus, but at a depth of three to six feet in the soil profile there is a light-colored layer of minerals, mainly carbonates of calcium and magnesium. This so-called lime layer is the limit to which moisture and the roots of plants penetrate. Below it the subsoil is dry. We are now in a true grassland climate; westward, in regions of still lower moisture, the lime layer will be progressively nearer the surface.

In central Nebraska the cover has changed also. Between the clumped formations of the midgrasses there is a lower level of vegetation, sods of buffalo grass and blue grama. These shortgrasses of the high plains extend their holdings eastward here to intermingle with the midgrasses. This, the *mixed prairie,* is a transition type between the moist prairies to the east and the dry plains to the west.

In a sense, the mixed prairie extends to the Rocky Mountains, since midgrasses can grow anywhere on sites with sufficient moisture. But another factor that makes a difference is buffalo grazing. There is universal competition for water, and where buffalo take off the annual crop of forage, shortgrasses do the better job. They spread, and the midgrasses give way. Thus, fronting the mountains, in a region averaging about fifteen inches of annual moisture, are the shortgrass plains.

Among the forbs of the midgrass prairie we now see silvery clumps of fringed sage, yellow heads of the annual sunflower, and rose-purple stalks of gayfeather. Snakeweed, phlox, locoweed, coralberry, pentstemon, ragwort, and rose mix with asters and goldenrods to bring color and variety to this grassland through the season. Locally adapted species and varieties of these herbs and shrubs grow with the mid-grasses in a belt from Texas to North Dakota and northwest into Saskatchewan.

In the southern half of this range we frequently encounter a plant that demands another look. It is something different in a range weed—purple to gray-green in color, with leaves bearing businesslike spiny tips. It will acquire the improbable name of Leavenworth eryngo, and neither the buffalo nor the white man's livestock will touch it. Of course, we do not have to be told that the bristling armament of the eryngo safeguards it against grazing.

Problem of the ages

Grazing animals are present in nearly every grassland. Hence all the plants that survive in such communities have the ability to live with the vegetation feeders. Some plants, like perennial grasses, are productive enough to sustain the annual cropping of their foliage and thrive in spite of it. Of course, their thrift does vary with changing conditions, but they do well on the average.

Some plants of the grassland are unpalatable, a characteristic they probably developed through the ages as the price of survival. This, too, is a matter of degree, and every kind of greenery probably is acceptable fare for some members of the animal community, whether the feeders be insects, bison, or some other.

Under truly arid conditions—that is, in deserts—much of the vegetation is heavily armed. It has to be, for many species, such as prickly pears and the yuccas, are quite edible, at least in their early growing stages. In arid lands, great family groups of woody and herbaceous plants have thorns, spines, and prickles that repel the hungry herb eaters that otherwise could destroy them.

But the eryngo does not belong to such a group. In fact, it is a member of the tender, nutritious (though a few are poisonous), and largely unarmed parsley family. With such origins, how did it develop stiff and spiny leaves like those of a yucca? Is this a defense against the bison—modern bison? Probably the best guess is no. This grazing-proofed

The attractive rose-purple gayfeather is native to the Texas coastal prairie, but it has many relatives—variously called gayfeathers, blazing stars, and button snakeroots—that in late summer are prominent features of plains and prairies everywhere. Grazing animals, including the bison, find these plants palatable.

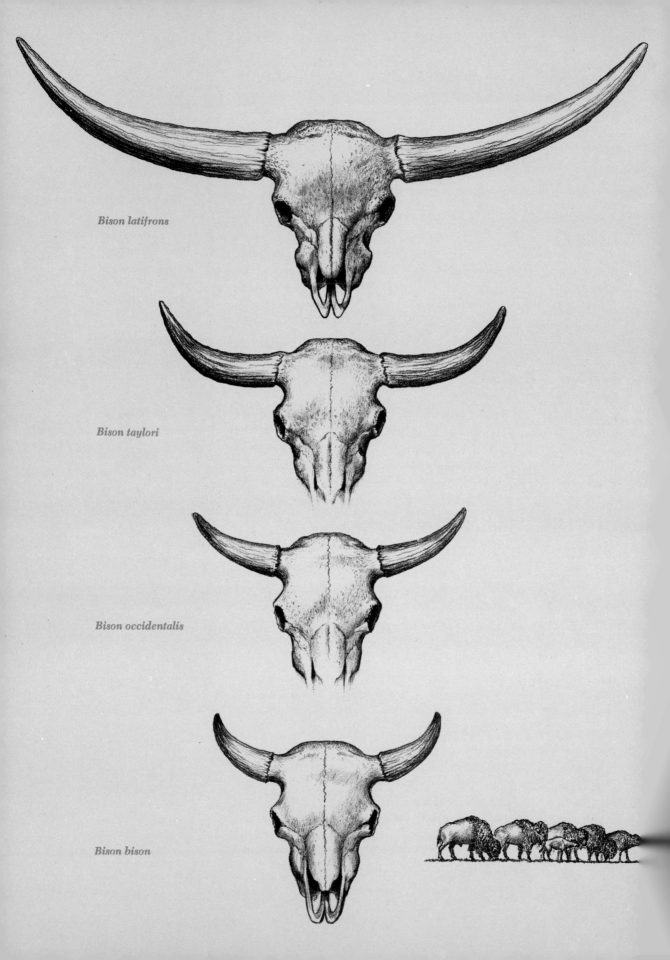

Bison latifrons

Bison taylori

Bison occidentalis

Bison bison

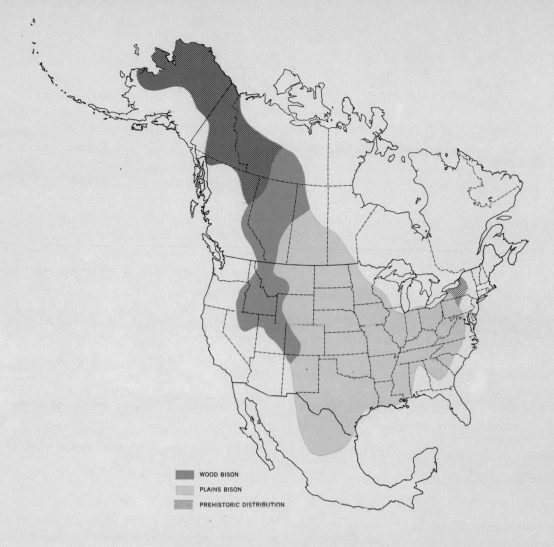

WOOD BISON

PLAINS BISON

PREHISTORIC DISTRIBUTION

The ancestry of the American buffalo forms a jigsaw puzzle from which many important pieces are still missing. The animal originated in Asia and first migrated to North America about a million years ago, when a huge amount of the earth's water was tied up in enlarged polar icecaps and continental glaciers. The ocean's level at that time was some three hundred feet lower than it is now. The Bering Strait between Alaska and Siberia was a low plain.

One of the first buffalo species to cross this ice-age bridge was *Bison latifrons*, which spread southward as far as Florida and Mexico, but which, for unknown reasons, passed into extinction. Two later species of buffalo, *Bison taylori* and *Bison occidentalis* (neither descended from *Bison latifrons*) flourished throughout much of the continent. Again from causes that are still mysterious, *Bison taylori* faded into extinction. *Bison occidentalis* survived, however, and is the ancestor of the modern buffalo, *Bison bison*. This species, as the map shows, gave rise to two races: the plains bison and the wood, or mountain, bison, a slightly larger, darker animal of the Canadian forests and the Rocky Mountains.

BISON OF THE NEW WORLD

eryngo could have taken a long time to develop, and that might leave out the bison.

To understand what happened to the eryngo, we probably need to look much further back into prehistory. During tens of millions of years, our continent has produced a vast parade of grazing animals, species that developed from primitive types, prospered for a period, and then became extinct. Ranges we would not recognize sustained countless numbers of *grazers*, which fed on the grasses, and *browsers*, which gained nourishment from woody plants. There was a long succession of thick-skinned beasts with horns or tusks. Some became the ancestors of recent elephants such as the mastodon and the mammoth. The horse underwent its racial development in North America. Then it invaded Asia, where it flourished, but its North American relatives died out. There were camels, giant elk, antelopelike creatures, and many more. Roughly a million years ago, the first migrations of early bison appeared in North America. The remains of about a dozen kinds have been found, but only two races— the plains bison and the wood bison—survived.

Which of all those early creatures might have fed on ancestral forms of this eryngo? We don't know, of course; but some certainly did, and we can be fairly sure how changes in the plant came about.

The process started because all living things are variable. No two plants of the early eryngo were exactly alike; some had tougher and sharper leaves than others. The plants with coarse leaves were not so frequently eaten by animals. Through long periods of time, the smooth and palatable plants were removed from the range, while the more tough and spiny ones lived to produce the seed for new generations.

As a result, here is our Leavenworth eryngo, with built-in protection against the buffalo. We might ask ourselves, why did not all plants of the grazing lands develop thorns? An obvious answer would seem to be that they did not need to. Each species has different requirements, and each developed a different design for survival. Every grass, forb, and shrub of this plant community has its own position to fill, not duplicating that of any other.

Over countless generations, the pressures of natural selection have caused eryngo, a member of the otherwise innocuous parsley family, to evolve the needle-sharp leaves that protect the plant from grazing animals.

The aging land

A careful look at the country over which we fly indicates that it is underlain by a wide variety of materials from which soil is being formed. In the badlands of the western Dakotas we see a rocky tableland being worn away by water and wind. In central Nebraska are hills of sand once transported by the wind. Great deposits of fertile wind-blown soils have helped to smooth the contours of the prairies and plains. In porous rocks deep under the dry mantle of the land, there is water which farmers and stockmen of the future will learn to bring up by means of windmills and other pumping devices.

The wind seems to blow constantly across this sea of grass. On the central and southern plains a dry blast of summer may, in a few days, parch everything in its path. Or a sudden "norther" may bring a cold front deep into Texas within a few hours. Again a moisture-laden air mass from the Gulf of Mexico may be cooled, and ten inches of rain dumped on the land overnight. The grassy sod may not hold under such a downpour, as the raw gullies and deep-worn stream beds show.

The grasslands are the birthplace of violent storms, tornadoes which may flatten a pathway eastward through forest edges. A bombardment of hail the size of hen eggs will maul whole flights of waterfowl or other migrant birds. Blizzards of the plains are the most savage on the continent. In the worst winters they may thin the ranks even of the hardy buffalo. By contrast, a *chinook*—a flow of warm air from the mountains—may melt a foot of snow overnight and send freshets romping across the sand bars of dry riverbeds.

For ages, the rivers of the grasslands have been carrying a silt load from the Rockies, depositing their burden in the channel as they dry up in summer. When its course has built too high, a stream is turned aside and seeks another way. In turn, this bed will be built up like the old one. Thus the land has come to slope outward from the mountains, from about four or five thousand feet above sea level at the Rocky Mountain foothills to three thousand feet at the eastern edge of the shortgrass plains. Large stretches of stream-borne silt and sand are bare to the wind.

There are new sights on the mixed prairies, such as the plentiful bare hills of the mound-building ant, which will be familiar in the drier country. And a new grazing animal is

The North Dakota prairie glows with reflected light against the dark backdrop of lowering storm clouds. The wind-rippled pothole in the foreground is ringed with moisture-loving whitetop grass. Common grasses of the hills beyond are native blue grama and needlegrass and the introduced bluegrass. The slopes are dotted with bleached clumps of last year's little bluestem.

43

BADLANDS NATIONAL MONUMENT

Unearthly landscapes of erosion-carved spires and pinnacles are the hallmark of the Dakota badlands. Under our National Park Service, 170 square miles of this unique region have been set aside in South Dakota as Badlands National Monument. Here, in addition to enjoying the spectacular rock formations for which the area is famous, you can see at first hand mixed-prairie country much as it appeared before the arrival of the white man. Many of the grasses and forbs described in this book grow here—annual sunflowers, blue grama, needle and thread, side-oats grama, little bluestem, and others. Grassland animals are well represented, too—prairie dogs and badgers, coyotes and cottontails, golden eagles and sharp-tailed grouse. Bison, once plentiful in the badlands, were wiped out during the great slaughter of the last century, but park officials have recently reintroduced them.

here, the pronghorn "antelope." It is not really an antelope, but it looks like one, and people will call it that. In midsummer the pronghorn bucks are gathering and herding their harems of does, accompanied by spring kids. Sometimes, a band unnoticed in the distance will flash brilliant white rump signals like a dozen mirrors as they course across the plain. Attending the pronghorns, as they do the buffalo, are the ever-present plains wolves and a smaller dog of open lands, the coyote, or brush wolf.

The shortgrass plains

Let us continue on and complete our quick look at the great central grassland. We soar away to the northwest, over the Dakota badlands and the rolling plains, extensive flats, and broken slopes of Montana and Saskatchewan. This is a land of grim winters, sparse rainfall, and shallow-rooted grasses.

The midgrass types do well here, though they are somewhat shorter and more scattered than in the central mixed prairie. Needlegrasses are widespread—three species, at least.

We note two kinds of wheatgrass, little bluestem, and in lesser amounts June grass, prairie dropseed, and a muhly grass. Small curly-leaved sedges add to the mixtures in many places. The common shortgrass is blue grama, which dominates the western portions of these northern plains. And beyond, the shortgrass sods give way to water-conserving bunch grasses and extensive stands of big sagebrush reaching far across Wyoming into the Great Basin.

The fringed sage lends its frosty gray-green tinge to miles of these rough, gravelly uplands. It is an aromatic half-shrub that one might see over an enormous area from Mexico to Alaska and on across Siberia and Eurasia. When in the dim past did this adventurous plant make that move across the Bering plain?

The imposing skyline of the Rocky Mountains is on our right as we speed south from Wyoming over the dry highlands of Colorado. We are in the rain shadow of the mountains, in a country of sparse forage, sage, dust, and buffalo. Even the stream margins here support but a scattered fringe of cottonwood and willow.

Here the tawny swards of buffalo grass and several kinds

This sight might have greeted a Pawnee hunting party on a hot July morning in the year 1491: herds of grazing bison dotting the shortgrass-clad eastern foothills of the Rocky Mountains. The tall mountains wring much of the rain from the moisture-laden winds blowing off the Pacific. These foothills thus lie within the "rain shadow" of the Rockies and have a semiarid climate in which the shortgrasses thrive.

THE SHORTGRASSES

In the semiarid grass country of
the high plains, and in the
driest regions of the prairies,
the shortgrasses dominate.
Growing no more than sixteen
inches high, these grasses
compete well under dry
conditions and under grazing;
whenever water becomes
plentiful, taller species crowd
them out. During the great
drought of the 1930s, buffalo
grass (*right*) and blue grama
(*far right*), both typical
shortgrass species, were able
to spread into areas formerly
occupied by taller grasses.
Blue grama forms a relatively
shallow but very dense sod.
Its twelve-inch flower stalks
each bear two or three
right-angled inch-long spikes.
Buffalo grass, often found mixed
with blue grama, grows only
four or five inches above the
ground. Its seed heads, unlike
those of blue grama, tend to
remain hidden within the
foliage.

The shortgrass country of the Southwest receives much of its sparse rainfall in short but incredibly heavy cloudbursts. Here you see great slanting columns of rain sweeping across a prairie of shortgrass studded with cholla cactus. If one of these storms catches you, you will find you cannot see more than a few feet through the torrential downpour, but moments later the storm will have passed and the sun will be shining brightly again.

of grama stretch away in gentle undulations that bake and shimmer in the sun's glare. Sections of horizon detach themselves in a distant mirage and stand high as flat-topped buttes and mesas that we know well enough are not there at all.

Buffalo use all the grasslands, but we suspect that here they are most at home. They are beasts of the sun country; sometimes it appears that a buffalo couldn't care less for shade. Between the aspen parklands of Canada and arid savannahs across the Rio Grande, there are millions of them. Commonly in sight are drifting dust clouds stirred by the loose herds as they move about to new pastures.

On this westward trip across the prairies and plains, we have seen increasing signs of our progress toward arid country. The prickly pear, a low cactus with waxy yellow flowers, is widespread, and the creamy white stalks of yucca stand high on areas of wind-drifted sand as far east as Michigan. Now similar species appear widely on the range. Here also, in areas closely cropped by buffalo, are fields of yellow broomweed and curlycup gumweed, species we saw commonly farther north. We notice that many of the plains forbs are yellow—sunflowers, butterweed, goldenweed, sundrop—richly complementing the pink-purple bloom of dotted gayfeather and the big blue sky overhead.

50

The shortgrasses of this region will be forage for the white man's cattle, especially buffalo grass and blue, black, hairy, and side-oats grama. Growing in heavily mineralized soil, the cured stands of grasses and herbs are prime feed throughout the dry, windy winters. The buffalo and antelope prosper on it.

South country

The ranges of shortgrass extend far southward, and on their western borders in New Mexico the buffalo grass gives way to galleta, which mixes with the gramas. There we see shrubs and other plants of semideserts on rougher and drier sites— big sage, saltbush, joint fir, and increasingly thriving stands of prickly pear and yucca.

Eastward, on the plains of Texas, we find buffalo grass again, and here the lowlands support an open chaparral of fine-leaved mesquite, live oak, and prickly evergreen shrubs. To the south and east in brushlands and river mottes bordering the Texas prairies, we encounter small groups of a piglike animal, the collared peccary, or javelina. These almost-pigs have three toes on the hind foot, rather than four. They live on acorns, pecans, chufas, and the fruits of prickly pear. These same habitats and food supplies support

The collared peccary, or javelina, inhabits the Texas brush savannahs that mark the southern limit of the central grasslands. A full-grown peccary stands close to two feet at the shoulder and weighs up to fifty pounds. Unlike a pig, the javelina has only three toes on each hind foot.

PRINCIPAL
GRASSLAND TYPES
OF THE
UNITED STATES
AND CANADA

SHORTGRASS PLAINS

COASTAL PRAIRIE

EASTERN PRAIRIE EDGE

TALLGRASS PRAIRIE

MIXED-GRASS PRAIRIE

SAGEBRUSH GRASSLAND

CALIFORNIA GRASSLAND

BUNCH-GRASS DESERT SHRUB

MINN.

WIS.

MICH.

IOWA

ILL.

IND.

OHIO

PA.

W.VA.

MO.

KY.

VA.

N.C.

TENN.

ARK.

S.C.

MISS.

ALA.

GA.

LA.

FLA.

flocks of the Rio Grande turkey. And here also is a small deer with spreading antlers, the Texas whitetail.

In eastern Texas the prairies have a familiar look, for here are tallgrasses and midgrasses common in the northern tall-grass prairie: big and little bluestem, Indian grass, and switch grass. A needlegrass not seen before, Texas needlegrass, is here, as are many others. This country is a mixing ground of grasses and forbs from all directions. An area of the coastal plain will be found to support nearly a thousand species of plants, of which more than 150 are grasses. The various gramas penetrate deeply from the west. Bluestems are conspicuous—broom sedge, silver, split-beard, seacoast. A cordgrass, sacahuiste, is widespread. Only a range expert can ever be familiar with this beautiful and varied flora.

Northward, blackland prairies lie between extensive belts of oak forest. The cross timbers of north Texas and Oklahoma are stands of small drought-adapted species, post oak and blackjack. These woodlands are interrupted by mixed-grass and tallgrass prairie types that continue northward into Kansas, Missouri, and Illinois. We saw them there on our way west.

We have made a great circuit of the grasslands. As we came south on the high plains from Canada, we progressed

Texas white-tailed deer, one of the smaller of our several races of whitetails, share with the peccary the brushy borders of the Texas grasslands. As in all deer, only the bucks are equipped with the bony, spreading antlers, which are dropped and replaced each year. The shed antlers are gnawed on by many species of calcium-craving rodents, including mice, ground squirrels, and porcupines.

from regions of lower to higher rainfall. In the cooler climate of the North, shortgrasses grow with fourteen inches of annual rainfall. The greater heat in southern ranges results in a higher evaporation rate, and more rain must fall for plants to have the same amount of available water. So, the shortgrasses of eastern Colorado must have seventeen inches, and those in Texas twenty-one.

This Rio Grande turkey displays the classic form of our wild turkeys—long, slim legs, spindle-shaped body, long tail, small head, and large eyes. The "style" of such a bird clearly sets it apart from the heavy-bodied domestic turkey. The long "beard" hanging down from the breast marks this bird as a tom.

Moist years and dry

What kind of weather are we having in this year 1491? For present purposes, let us assume that it is neither extremely dry nor extremely moist.

Of course, nothing stays "average" for very long, especially weather. In the grasslands there will be years with more than usual rainfall, then other periods of parching drought. Often the trends come in a series of years during which the extreme conditions build up in their effects. The well-organized vegetation responds predictably to such change.

In low areas of the tallgrass prairie, a series of wet years means fewer fires, perhaps none at all. Tree seedlings spread out from woodland borders, invading grassy sods. Some move downgrade from rocky slopes and oak-mantled ridges,

where there is little grass to burn and where tree roots go far down to water. Woody plants march into the openings from Minnesota to the Gulf of Mexico. The Texas chaparral encroaches on the bluestem and sacahuiste of the coastal plain.

Inevitably the dry years come, and this process is reversed. Where woody plants have occupied droughty places in favorable years, the advance guard of trees and shrubs become unhealthy and off-color. Insects plague them, and in time they die. On richer lands fires rage through the tallgrass to open up the edges of forest and brush again.

From Illinois to Colorado, other changes are taking place. In several years of continuous drought, the tallgrasses lose ground far and wide. Western wheatgrass and other midgrass types become more plentiful in the eastern prairies. But they lose their drier holdings in the central mixed-grass region as shortgrasses take over.

Summing it up, the plant communities of the entire grassland tend to shift eastward for a few years. And on the plains themselves the sods thin out as various grasses assume more commonly a bunch-grass habit. In exposing bare ground between the clumps, Nature has brought about a fallowing for water conservation.

In all their phases, the drought-stricken grasslands are more heavily stocked with the temporary cover of annual grasses and forbs. These are the same plants we see growing in the edges of trails and wallows of the buffalo—the filmy panicles of the tumbleweed witch grass, slender bunches of six-weeks fescue, the silvery plumes of foxtail barley, and prairie three-awn, whose sticky fruits cling to our clothing as we follow the trekking bison. Conspicuous forbs of this disturbed-soil community are the annual sunflower, plains bee balm, broomweed, woolly plantain, and buffalo bur. These plants have an important job to do when drought, trampling, or digging lays bare the ground surface. They hold soil against the action of wind and water until perennial weeds and grasses reestablish their more permanent cover. This recovery starts when a drought is broken and rainfall returns to something approaching "normal."

A head of annual sunflower, ornamented with a cucumber beetle, turns toward the warm prairie sun. This tall forb is characteristic of sites disturbed by buffalo.

Creatures

of the Grass

The prairies and plains are lands of extremes, the home of life communities long adapted to all conditions that occur. In progressively changing forms, many living things have been in the grasslands since the earth's crust wrinkled and the Rocky Mountains were thrust skyward some fifty million years ago. Ever after, the north-south ridges fended west winds upward and cooled them, releasing their moisture on the forests of upper slopes. The creation of a "rain shadow" to the east left the plains dry and set the course for a countless number of species that had to adapt or perish. Many disappeared, but others are with us still. Plants and animals of the grassland have special kinds of fitness, or they would have been drop-outs long ago.

Let us look more closely at some of these inhabitants of the vast mid-region of North America. We must see how they live and what has made them successful in meeting the challenges of competition and changing conditions.

The herders

Of the hoofed mammals in North America in 1491, only two are typical of grasslands: the buffalo and the pronghorn. Their distribution overlaps broadly on the plains, although the bison extends far to the east, while the pronghorn is exclusively western.

Nebraska is roughly the center of bison distribution. On the Atlantic side of the continent, buffalo bands use grassy openings deep into the broad-leaved forests of the East. There are some buffalo in western Pennsylvania and in various locations south to Georgia. In Kentucky and Tennessee their grazing helps the periodic fires maintain isolated but extensive prairies. In that region, where waters heavily charged with minerals reach the surface, the ground is worn bare around long-used "licks." It is characteristic of forested country that, as parent materials of the soil break down and become soluble, the compounds are steadily washed away by the deep percolating waters. As a result, in such habitats the bison seek out these mineral supplements wherever they may be found. There is no such need in the dry West, where soluble salts accumulate in the soil. "Alkali" is everywhere, and these mineral salts are part of every bit of forage or drink of water.

No doubt the buffalo browse woody plants on forest edges, but they have another habit that gives advantage to the grass. We see evidence of this clearly where grassland joins stands of lodgepole or ponderosa pine at the foot of western mountains. There, with great enjoyment, buffalo despoil young pines that have become established in the sods. Watching an old bull feed in a stand of four-foot ponderosas on a lower slope of South Dakota's Black Hills leaves no doubt about it.

Occasionally he turns aside from his grazing to rub his head vigorously against the branched stem of a young pine. Starey-eyed and stupid-looking, he stands and scrubs away —in total disregard for the welfare of future forests. In turn, on one side and then the other, he hooks a horn around

The largest and most spectacular creature of the grasslands—indeed, of North America—is the majestic American bison, or buffalo. Enormous herds of bison once roamed the heartland of the continent.

These young ponderosa pines had spearheaded a forest invasion of the grass, but the mauling and head scratching of the bison have killed most of the young trees. The next grass fire will wipe out their remains. The constant rubbing and "horning" of the animals destroy even full-grown trees by stripping their bark.

the base of the tree and strips upward. It's a great job of head scratching, but the tree is ruined.

Now it is evident why we see bulls (they do it more than cows) walking around with green branches hanging on their horns. Hundreds of small pines are shredded and killed. They become tinder-dry and burn with fury in the next grass fire, which may get hot enough to take out the whole stand. Thus, because their heads itch, buffalo manage the grass and improve their own range.

Westward from the Wyoming plains, a few buffalo find sparse and poorly watered pastures across sagebrush and wheatgrass country to eastern Oregon. Probably some, or

all, of these animals are mountain buffalo. This race lives in the Rockies from the high parks of Colorado northward into the mountain valleys of British Columbia. From there it spreads out across Canadian parklands and muskegs, where future white men will know it as the wood bison.

The range of the plains buffalo narrows in the South. A few of these animals get into western New Mexico, and in west Texas herds commonly move across the Rio Grande for wintering. But in east Texas they do not go south of the blackland prairies. On the coastal plain there is a grassland with no hoofed creature to crop its annual growth of forage.

This bull bison jauntily wears a sprig of foliage behind one horn—evidence that he has been scratching his head by hooking and tearing up shrub invaders of the grassland edge. In this way the big animals help to favor their own pasturage in that "zone of tension" between the grassland and the encroaching forest.

BUFFALO SUMMER

It is late June in the grass country, and the summer phase of the buffalo's life is under way. The shedding of winter wool is well along, and the cows have their new orange-red calves. A cow band (*left*), including juvenile males up to three and four years old, is gathered at a wallow that has seen use for many years. At other dust "pans" in the vicinity are bachelor groups of breeding bulls that have spent the winter apart. They will join the cow bands about mid-July, when the running season begins. After this, any cow in breeding condition will be closely followed by a bull, and "tending" pairs (*following two pages*) will be a common sight on the outskirts of every band until late August.

Bulls commonly contend for the rights to a cow, and the large, strong, and socially dominant animals are most successful. Usually a show of horns is all that is necessary to discourage a presumptive suitor, but desperate fights sometimes develop between superior animals. The bulls roar, paw the earth, and stalk together for a heaving, shoving head-to-head encounter (*below*). Although much of the fighting is ritual, occasionally animals are killed. The cows take no interest in such proceedings, and will simply be escorted away by the successful bull.

The buffalo bands remain mixed through the fall, after which older bulls usually separate for wintering. The calves, which weigh twenty-five to forty pounds at birth, shed their reddish wool at about three months of age and assume the dark color of an adult buffalo. By fall a healthy youngster may have increased to four hundred pounds, and its coat will be long, shaggy, and thickened with wool against the rigors of the cold season on the plains.

A bull exhausted by the stresses and competition of the running season may wander alone far from the bands for a late-summer rest and regaining of weight. Old animals sometimes retire to a solitary life until the end of their days. Bulls are ready to mate at the age of five, but most of the breeding is done by animals from age six to about fourteen. Cow buffalo have been found healthy and bearing calves at more than thirty years of age.

The bull buffalo is considerably larger than his mate: full-grown males stand six feet at the shoulder and weigh upwards of a ton, while cows reach only half that weight. This tending pair is accompanied by the cow's spring calf.

Though often called an antelope, the pronghorn is the sole living member of an exclusively American family of animals distinct from the true antelopes of Africa. Both male and female bear horns, but those of the buck, shown here, are markedly longer than the doe's and normally exceed his ears in length. The buck is further characterized by his black muzzle and neck patches, which are absent in his mate.

The coursers

Pronghorns are at home from the mixed prairies west. They inhabit intermountain grasslands and arid brush country to the Central Valley of California. From north to south their range extends from the plains of Alberta and Saskatchewan deep into Mexico.

This creature thrives under the brilliant high-plains sun. Yet, more often than the buffalo, one of them will be seen lying, head up and alert, in the shade of an isolated tree. Is it keeping cool, or is it seeking the camouflage of the tree shadow? It would be interesting to know.

In spring, on a sagebrush and wheatgrass range in Wyoming, we can learn something of the pronghorn. Let us watch a doe as she feeds and surveys the landscape from a hillcrest. Unlike a deer, she does not use cover for concealment. Hers is the open ground, where danger makes itself known far off. We see readily, however, that the whites and browns of the pronghorn color pattern blend

70

well with the vegetation. This is true both summer and winter.

Several hundred yards away this doe has two well-separated kids (sometimes only one) lying low in the vegetation. At intervals she visits them so they can nurse, then leaves quickly. For a week after birth the kids hide, and then they begin to accompany their mother. Rapidly they acquire the endurance and amazing speed of their kind.

Some miles away there are flashes of brilliant white, and we move on to investigate. Now we see them—several pronghorn bucks speeding away from a group of Indians and dogs. The bucks have erected the hairs of their white rump rosettes, and this serves as a signal to others. Eventually they stop on a rise, where all simultaneously shake themselves, and the signals disappear.

The Indians are afoot and slow-moving. However, they have managed to kill one of the bucks; they are dressing it out, slashing the hide and dismembering the carcass rapidly with strokes of leaf-shaped flints. They have learned that the pronghorn is full of curiosity and lives by seeing and investigating all that goes on in its wide-open world. So, a stick with a tuft of feathers waved above the grass, or an

During the first few days of its life, this newborn five-pound pronghorn kid will depend for its survival largely on its instinctive ability to lie perfectly still in the grass except when its mother visits it for nursing. Yet at the age of only four days this seemingly helpless little creature will be able to outrun a man, and within a week it will start journeying with its mother.

COURSERS OF THE PRAIRIES

To a certain extent the ponderous bison can rely upon its sheer bulk to protect it against its natural enemies, but not so the hundred-pound pronghorn. It must rely upon flight, and everything about the animal suggests speed. Its legs are heavily built, its lungs and windpipe are large, and its heart is twice as big as that of an ordinary animal its size. Thirty miles an hour is an easy lope for a pronghorn, and forty-five is not unusual. If pressed, the creature can hit a speed of sixty miles an hour and maintain it for three or four minutes, covering the ground in great twenty-foot bounds.

Although pronghorns eat some grass, especially during the early spring, they are primarily browsers of weeds and shrubs. Sagebrush (above) is a favorite food.

A pronghorn buck, the animal at the far left in the upper picture, has assembled a respectable-sized harem of five does, accompanied here by two kids. He will guard the does against challengers through autumn. With the coming of winter, however, all the animals will regather into mixed herds such as the one shown in the lower picture.

Two pronghorn bucks (left) lock horns during the late-summer breeding season. Each buck tries to assemble a harem of a dozen or more does, which he attempts to keep together as a group even after mating is completed.

Not a full-time plains dweller like the bison and pronghorn, the magnificent American elk, or wapiti, nevertheless forages in the grass country bordering forests and mountains. This is the largest of our native deer: a bull may stand five feet at the shoulder and weigh eight hundred pounds. The elk originally flourished throughout most of the continent, but now it is found in substantial numbers only in the large wilderness ranges of the West.

Indian lying on his back and kicking his feet in the air, will gradually "toll" the pronghorn to close range, where a well-placed arrow can kill or disable it.

It has been implied here that only two hoofed mammals really belonged to the grassland biome. That is not quite correct. On the dry plain of California, which surrounds tule, or bulrush, marshes along the rivers, the pronghorn shares its wealth of forage with a big-game species peculiar to that area—the valley, or tule, elk.

This elk does belong to the grasslands, and it will find the going hard in the period of settlement. By the middle of the twentieth century it will be gone from its native range and restricted to a few southern California ranches.

Of course, other elk make extensive use of grasslands, but most commonly near forested and mountain country, to which they like to retire during the hot months of summer. They cannot withstand heat like the bison and pronghorn. Elk are the most versatile feeders of all North American deer, consuming a wide variety of grasses and other herbs, as well as browse of many kinds.

Elk and white-tailed deer are found throughout the eastern forests, and they share the wooded stream bottoms of the grass region. From Minnesota to the Dakota badlands and Black Hills west, the rugged country and mountains are home to the mule deer and, again, the elk. Both need brushlands, forests, and meadows.

The two most typical big-game animals of the prairies and plains region show protective characteristics found in grassland species the world over. The buffalo is gregarious; it associates in a socially organized herd, which ensures a high measure of security from its principal enemy, the wolf. In the pronghorn's smaller groups there may be similar advantages, but it survives principally by being keen of eye and swift of foot.

Life underground

Anyone who observes the life of grasslands for very long will be impressed with the way events repeat themselves. A particular kind of animal is likely to be seen doing the same thing almost every day at a given time. For example, during the midday hours we can expect the buffalo to be standing quietly or lying with tucked legs, chewing its cud.

74

At sunset, when vesper sparrows call and nighthawks buzz and boom overhead, the buffalo bands are on the move, grazing briskly.

Many creatures are abroad at night. Others are at their daily business in full sunlight, and among these none is so evident as the ground squirrels. These burrowing rodents are with us in every part of the grass country, commonly two or three kinds in any one locality. They are tillers of the sun-baked ground; they loosen, aerate, and mix the soil. On sites of their disturbance, annual forbs appear—sunflower, thistle, woolly plantain, ragweed, peppergrass, smartweed, to name a few. These and various grasses bear seed crops that feed such creatures as harvester and mound-building ants, seed-eating birds, and, of course, the rodents themselves.

A ground squirrel we saw immediately after reaching the prairies seems to be on hand to greet us everywhere. It is chipmunk-sized and conspicuously striped in dark brown and buff, with every alternate light stripe broken into dots. This animal will be called the striped ground squirrel, or thirteen-lined spermophile. Like other small creatures that sit up and whistle in the meadows, it will be simply a "gopher" to many people.

This particular gopher has a wide domain from the prairies of Michigan and Indiana to the plains of Alberta and south to Kansas. Even these are not the limits of the species, for to the south and west there are other striped ground squirrels different enough to be recognized as separate races, or subspecies.

The winding, shallow burrows of this animal are not marked with piles of fresh soil; the entrance holes are hidden by vegetation, and earth from the underground passages is scattered. What such a home is like becomes more evident when a badger rips it open for twenty feet of winding trench in his hope of cornering its occupant. Here is a chamber lined with a thick nest of grasses; another is a storehouse for a wide variety of seeds and roots.

If we watch a spermophile carefully as he moves over the paths around his entrance holes, we get a clue to the nature of many kinds of ground squirrels; in fact, many kinds of rodents. They live well on grains, tubers, fruits, and leafy vegetables, but they also have a well-developed taste for meat in many forms. This one sits up beside a bunch of little bluestem, turning something over in its forepaws. It is ex-

What was that? Alert for danger, a bright-eyed thirteen-lined ground squirrel stands up and cranes its neck for a better view. If it spots a predator—and it is subject to many—it will turn and dive for the safety of its burrow.

pertly shucking the hard parts from a grasshopper, which it proceeds to eat with gusto. Later we see it actively at work on an ant hill. Rapidly it licks up the ants, as well as the eggs and pupae the seemingly frantic insects are carrying out of their underground home. This reminds us that we have noticed various kinds of ant hills widely in our travels. Ants surely must rank with gophers as tillers of the grassland soils.

Here and there around the spermophile diggings we find the wing coverts of ground beetles and the legs of crickets. There are occasions when the little assassin will come back with cheek pouches bulging with tender young mice from a raided nest. And it is not by chance that we see ground squirrels foraging around the remains of a buffalo.

Some of the naturalists of future years will be surprised to learn that this and numerous other rodents of the grass country never, or seldom, take a drink. Observers will say that these creatures get all their necessary water from their food, which is true.

Of course, the juices of succulent plants and fruits are a source of water, but this is not the whole story. In the animal body, products of digestion are circulated to the tissues, where they are used inside individual cells for growth and energy. This process of assimilation involves a combination of the food-fuels with oxygen from the lungs. It is a kind of internal combustion, and a by-product of the reaction is water. In this way water is acquired even from dry foods. Creatures in dry climates are so adapted

A trio of month-old thirteen-lined ground squirrels frolic under their mother's watchful eye in front of an artificial burrow. The female brings forth from five to thirteen young in a grass-lined underground nursery (*opposite page*). **This creature, common throughout the grasslands, has a distinctive dot-and-dash color pattern that makes it easy to recognize.**

that their bodies lose a minimum of moisture; they sweat little, and their urine is concentrated. This makes it possible for some species to get by largely or wholly on *metabolic water*, water produced by their body chemistry.

Food stores of the striped ground squirrel are used in early spring and at other times of scarcity, such as drought. Like many of its kindred, this ground squirrel needs no food in winter. From October to April it is rolled up in a nest in an earth-sealed chamber, living very slowly indeed; for this is the deep sleep of *hibernation*. The animal's temperature drops, its pulse rate slows, and it breathes only a few times a minute. The fat stored last fall provides all the energy it needs until the spring awakening.

Then follows a time of great activity: it is the breeding season. A brood of six to ten is brought forth in May or June, and the young become independent in summer.

For many ground squirrels the summer-winter schedule is different in more arid ranges. The period of inactivity, which is in the hot, dry weeks of summer, is known as *estivation* rather than hibernation. Animals normally estivate after they have built up body fat by plentiful feeding earlier in the growing season. In some areas the same ground squirrels hibernate in winter and then have a short sleep during the hot months. Many western species become dormant about midsummer, remain "out of it" for more than half the year, then emerge in late winter for breeding. Ground squirrels in the South commonly do not hibernate, but simply hole up for periods of bad weather.

Gopher world

In the eastern region of true prairies one frequently sees a larger relative of the striped species: Franklin's ground squirrel, or the gray gopher. This one likes the vicinity of oak groves and brushy edges. It gathers in colonies that are easy to recognize by the piles of soil thrown out by the excavators. Something we have learned to associate with tallgrass areas is the clear and birdlike whistle of this rodent.

Overlapping the prairie country of the Franklin's ground squirrel and extending across the needlegrass region of the North is the realm of a truly abundant grassland rodent, the Richardson's ground squirrel. Sometimes we count dozens or even hundreds to the acre as each squirrel stands high on its hind feet beside a mound of fresh earth. It is evident why this creature will be called "picket pin." An alarm spreads across the colony in a series of loud whistles, and the animals dive for their burrows with a great switching of tails. Underground, the tunnel may go down five feet and have a total length of fifty feet or more.

The rat-sized Franklin's and Richardson's ground squirrels are fairly representative of many more species and races scattered through the large and small grasslands of the West. For example, the Columbian ground squirrel is typical of the prairies covering a great deposit of wind-blown soil in eastern Washington; but it also does well in rocky and forested mountain habitats. The widespread California ground squirrel is similarly versatile, and for a gopher it does an exceptionally good job of climbing trees. Early in the twentieth century, it will be discovered that this common ground squirrel of California's Central Valley is a carrier of diseases infectious in human beings, notably bubonic plague and tularemia.

America's wildlife includes nearly two dozen species of ground squirrels, adapted to a wide variety of habitats. The Uinta ground squirrel (*left*) is not abundant, but it is found in cool upland meadows from Montana south into Utah. The more common Richardson's ground squirrel (*right*) is found widely across northern grasslands and brushlands from the Rockies to the Mississippi River.

Prairie-dog town

By far the most characteristic burrowing rodent of the
plains and mixed prairies is the black-tailed prairie dog,
whose bare, mound-dotted "towns" we see over hundreds
of square miles. This large nonhibernating ground squirrel
(well, not quite a ground squirrel, but who would know
that in 1491?) is thoroughly entangled in the web of relationships that binds together all living things of the grassland community.

Through practice, we shall come to look for prairie dogs
in areas heavily grazed by buffalo, where the taller grasses
have been thinned out and the range is largely taken over
by buffalo grass and gramas. In a heavily populated dog
town the foot-high craters that mark burrow entrances are
commonly ten to thirty feet apart. There is bare ground
around the mounds, and many trails crisscross the heavily
worked vegetation. The rodents feed on both grasses and
forbs of various kinds, and their disturbance of the sod
promotes the growth of the annual *invaders*, plants that
characteristically grow on bare soil. The towns are a favorite resort of buffalo because the bare, dusty areas are an
invitation to wallow almost anywhere—and wallowing is
the comfort and joy of a buffalo's life from the time he is a
red calf to "retirement" age. An old loner bull wants nothing
better than a well-worn dog town.

On a sunny day we can spend an hour among the
prairie dogs and nearly always see something new. Their

way of life is closely adjusted to the grassland. The mounded burrow entrance undoubtedly helps prevent flooding in a downpour, but this animal has another kind of flood insurance. The main tunnel may go down steeply for ten feet or more; then one or more lateral passages turn up, forming a pocket that will trap air even when the rest of the burrow is filled with water. There are nesting chambers stuffed with grasses and, as is common with many burrowing animals, tunnels where droppings are deposited. These are cleaned out on occasion.

By midsummer the young are well grown and traveling from one den to another. Sometimes we see a family group of four or five sitting erect on a mound, surveying the world carefully before heading out to feed. Frequently one will turn and make mouth contact with another. Later observers will call this "kissing."

The shadow of a passing turkey vulture sends some of the dogs into their holes, while others bark sharply and sit high on the alert. Then we notice the shape of the prairie dog: its head is slightly rounded and the eyes are set high. It can see over the edge of its mound with very little of its head showing. The animals that dived for safety are up and looking about almost at once. They come out and move cautiously on their paths to clumps of grass and forbs and begin to eat. A stem or leaf is grasped in one paw and fed into the rapidly working jaws. Sometimes we see a prairie dog scraping earth backward toward its mound and then packing the loose soil by pressure with its head.

In their heyday before the coming of white settlers to the western plains, the bustling, gregarious prairie dogs built "towns" that in terms of population and area, at least, put human efforts to shame. One such town in Texas at the turn of the century was estimated to cover 25,000 square miles and house 400 million of the rodents. Prairie dogs were not the only residents of their towns. Burrowing owls, among other "squatters," frequently made themselves at home in unused burrows and occasionally helped themselves to young prairie dogs. The lumbering badger (far left) and the lithe black-footed ferret (far right) posed more serious threats: at the approach of either of these enemies, the dogs would dive underground, but the ferret was slender enough to follow, and the badger was well adapted to wholesale excavation to reach the holed-up rodents. Despite the attentions of these and a host of other predators, literally billions of prairie dogs inhabited the grasslands as recently as the last century, but intensive extermination campaigns by man have now reduced the great prairie-dog nation to a few scattered colonies.

Burrowing owls are competent tunnelers in their own right, but usually they will set up housekeeping in a ready-made burrow abandoned by a prairie-dog family. The long-legged little owls feed on mice, insects, small snakes and lizards, and young prairie dogs. However, the dogs compensate by stealing eggs from the owls and occasionally eating young owls.

Perched on the edge of what appears to be an old mound is a creature seen frequently around the towns, a small long-legged owl. The burrowing owl nests underground in a chamber of the prairie dog's tunnel. Long ago its ancestors joined the community of the grasslands. An occasional bullsnake or prairie rattler may bring alarm and consternation to the dogs as it invades the tunnels for its own unwelcome purpose. The rodents know well what their neighbors are about. They pay little attention to a box turtle that is clumsily prying over a buffalo chip to pick up darkling beetles and other small prey that may be underneath. Before winter the turtle will bury itself in a pocket of an old burrow and become inactive.

At intervals a prairie dog throws its head violently up and backward, forefeet in the air, and utters a characteristic call, *whee-ool*, before dropping back to all fours. The call probably forewarns footloose neighbors that this part of the range is occupied. Family groups seem to have the town divided up into private holdings, much as do the male prairie chickens on the booming grounds and male songbirds that sing over their territories on the grassland. Within the territory the old male, one or more females, and the young of the year appear to use the various burrows at will. Trespassers are repelled, especially by the male.

Prairie dogs are among the most influential creatures of the grass country. They bring subsoil up and spread it on the surface, where it breaks down into soluble forms of plant food. Their burrows conduct air underground and make oxygen available to the great host of microbial life and other small living things that contribute to the enrichment and mellowing of soils. The deep layers are loosened and fertilized with deposits of vegetation, droppings, and topsoil.

The vegetation itself is considerably affected by the joint action of buffalo and prairie dog. Many animals of this community are dependent on the seeds, tubers, roots, and foliage of those early weed stages—call them annual, temporary, pioneer, or invader stages—in the succession of grassland vegetation. As we have seen, these are the plants that move in and heal over areas of disturbed or denuded soil. The burrowing rodents and mound-building ants, and such heavy grazers as bison and grasshoppers, are unceasingly at work renewing such conditions.

82

Prairie dogs, among the most social of rodents, live together in large family units, each with its definite territory in the town. Clan members seem to delight in kissing and grooming each other. They help each other dig burrows, and they peaceably share grazing rights, although outsiders are promptly ejected. The prairie dogs also cooperate in guarding against hawks, coyotes, and other enemies: a single warning bark will send every dog within earshot diving for underground safety.

Home in the sod

It seems that one can know a few kinds of animals only by their signs. Already in the easternmost prairies we noticed mounds of loose earth here and there, as though the soil had been pushed up from below. These mounds, a foot or two across, fall into two patterns, round and fan-shaped. Both are made by creatures that spend practically their entire lives underground.

One of them, the mole, is not a rodent but an insectivore. Gray-brown, chunky, and spindle-shaped, the mole weighs about five ounces. By sheer strength it shoves loose earth from its tunnels straight up through a hole to form those circular mounds. More commonly it wedges its way through the fibrous root mass of the topsoil, heaving the sod into long, winding ridges that are visible where the grass is short.

In these subsurface wanderings the velvety furred mole is searching for white grubs, earthworms, millipedes, beetles, sowbugs, and other living fare. It searches by scent and touch, for its pinhead eyes are closed by permanently sealed lids. We might expect this in a creature that lives in darkness.

From the eastern forest region, the mole continues its range out onto the southern half of the prairies, principally in rich, moist soils. It does not belong to the high, dry grasslands.

But the plains pocket gopher certainly does. This rodent has digging habits somewhat like the mole; it made those fan-shaped mounds in sandy areas south of Lake Michigan, and it does quite well in fine-textured soils throughout the central grasslands. It has relatives that extend the pocket-gopher world across the semiarid ranges of the West.

The pocket gopher is not the kind of gopher we discussed before, but it does have pockets. These are two external fur-lined cheek pouches; that is, they fold in from the outside. They are used to carry food or nesting material. The chisellike incisor teeth are always in front of the lips, which turn in and close behind them. This is an arrangement that allows the pocket gopher to cut its gritty food—roots, tubers, bulbs, and other plant parts—without getting dirt in its mouth. These continuously growing teeth are worn away rapidly, as much as fourteen inches a year for the lower pair.

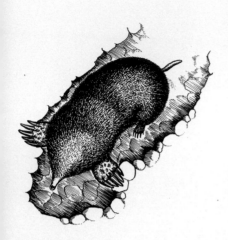

Powerful shovellike forelegs, a velvety coat that brushes smooth either way, skin-covered eyes and no external ears, keen senses of touch and smell —thus has Nature equipped the mole for life in its dark underground world. Spurred by a voracious appetite, the mole tunnels tirelessly all through the year in search of its food, consuming up to half its body weight in earthworms, grubs, and insects every twenty-four hours.

The pocket gopher is well
prepared for life below
the surface, but its mode
of living differs from that
of the mole in several
respects. The mole tunnels
by forcing the soil upward
or to the side; the pocket
gopher, an excavator,
loosens the earth with
claws and teeth and
pushes it out through
a vertical shaft with its
head. The mole feeds on
earthworms and insects;
the pocket gopher is a
vegetarian. The mole eats
as it goes; the pocket
gopher lays up stores
of neatly harvested
roots and stems. A
final distinguishing
characteristic of the
pocket gopher is the pair
of special fur-lined
storage pouches in its
cheeks, which give the
unusual rodent its
common name.

Like the mole, the pocket gopher has a fine, silky fur. Why do the true creatures of the underground have this kind of fur? Surely it must wear well and protect them effectively in contact with the moist earth. It is an example of how the same environment has brought about the same adaptation in distantly related animals.

The front feet of the pocket gopher also resemble those of the mole; they are short, heavily clawed, and spadelike. When boring through the ground, this powerful one-pound animal places its head and front feet against a plug of loose soil, and, using only the hind feet for traction, bulldozes the load up and out onto its surface dump. No other digger of the rodent clan can quite match this one. The burrows of a single animal may be five hundred feet in length and cover an acre of ground. To maintain its prodigious efforts, the pocket gopher requires about half its own weight in food per day. It needs to live amid plenty!

Millions of little teeth

Everywhere the grasslands are populated with small mice. Mostly they are night-active, or *nocturnal*, and live underground. Typical of the tallgrass and midgrass prairies is the prairie deer mouse, a neat white-bellied mouse with large, shiny shoe-button eyes. Another race of the same species lives in forested areas to the north. There are locally adapted varieties of the deer mouse in nearly every conceivable habitat in North America.

The prairie deer mouse lives in burrows in the sod, where females bring forth their first litters as early as March. Some of these young will be breeding at two months of age and contribute to a large population build-up before autumn. Like all small plant-eating animals, this one has a host of enemies that feed on it, but there must be mice left over for another year.

The prairie deer mouse garners the weed seeds and small fruits of the grassland. A close look at its cheek teeth would tell us that they are designed for mashing up seeds; they are blunt and have rounded tubercles. Even carnivores such as the bear and raccoon have similar molar teeth, since they feed on a mixed diet including nuts and fruits, as well as animals of various kinds.

During winter we see small squirrellike tracks in the

The diet of the dainty little prairie deer mouse consists mainly of seeds, small nuts, and fruit pits, but during the summer this vegetarian fare is supplemented with caterpillars, beetles, centipedes, and, occasionally, other mice. Where deer mice abound, their avid seed gathering can check the spread of the forest into the grassland by preventing the establishment of seedling trees.

86

snow, leading from one projecting seed.head of the prairie forbs to another. They show clearly what the deer mouse is about. Yet underground, in a chamber of the burrow system, the frugal animal may have, still unused, a pint of seeds left over from autumn storage. In the cold season it is common for a dozen or more mice to share the same quarters. Of course, in spring they scatter out for breeding.

The prairie deer mouse holds strictly to open ground, but every area of brush or woods is inhabited by a closely similar deer mouse species, the white-footed mouse. This one is equally at home on the forest floor or in the treetops, where it lives in hollows or old bird nests and feeds on nuts and seeds. As compared with the prairie deer mouse, it has a slightly longer tail, its ears are a bit larger, and there are minor color differences. Yet individual specimens can be found, especially young ones, which are not clearly one or the other.

How do small variations in form and structure make such a great difference in the habits of two creatures? We suppose that, for all time to come, biologists will wish they knew more about such things.

If we poke about in lush stands of grass, we commonly find at ground level a maze of miniature tunnellike paths winding among the stems and rootstocks. There is ample evidence that many sharp teeth are doing the job, cutting vegetation and maintaining the tunnels.

It is the work of the meadow mouse, or prairie vole. This chunky rodent is not a handsome sprite like the deer mouse. Its legs and tail are short, and its eyes small. It is of a solid color, gray with a wash of golden brown on the *guard hairs* of the back—those large, coarse hairs that protrude through a mammal's underfur. A look at its cheek teeth betrays its food habits, for they have a flattened grinding surface patterned with triangles of sharp enamel ridges. In some ways these teeth are like those of the bison, and indeed they are for the same purpose: grinding grass and other vegetation. This abundant leaf-eating mouse will find a bountiful living in the white man's hayfields and close-growing grain.

In winter the tunnel systems of the meadow mouse are well protected by snow, and the animal makes globular aboveground nests of dry grasses. These nests are abandoned for underground quarters when the snow melts. Through the growing season, a rapid succession of large litters are born to stock anew the vast expanse of grassland with its huge resource of growing plants.

Although the plains harvest mouse (*top*) closely resembles the common house mouse, it is a native American, while the house mouse is a European immigrant that came across with the first white settlers. The prairie meadow mouse (*bottom*) is, strictly speaking, not a mouse but rather a member of the abundant and widespread vole subfamily, stockier than mice and with shorter tails and less prominent ears.

87

A one-ounce tiger of the grass-root jungle, the grasshopper mouse (*top*) is a voracious predator that trails and devours not only grasshoppers but a variety of other small creatures as well, including scorpions, small lizards, and other mice. Strolling through grass country at twilight, you might easily mistake a meadow jumping mouse (*bottom*) for a frog or toad as it bounds away from you in prodigious five- to ten-foot leaps. Seeds, fruits, and insects form its diet.

The place of the prairie vole in the grassland community is impressed upon us as we sit on a grassy slope, watching the life about us. A sparrow hawk—actually a stylish robin-sized falcon—comes winging along at a height of a dozen feet. Suddenly it flips over and dives straight for the ground. We can almost hear the thud as it disappears into the grass. Then, with a rapid beat of its pointed wings, it rises from the worn stand of last year's bluestem. Dangling from its talons is the short-tailed stubby form of a meadow mouse.

In the central plains, a region that will someday be western Kansas and Nebraska, we find other small night-active rodents. They are representative of many similar species or varieties that inhabit the grass and semiarid brushlands to the north, south, and west. To see and become familiar with the mouselike creatures of the grasslands, we need to be abroad at night, as they are, and we must watch quietly in many situations.

In the glow of moonlight a tiny elfin pocket mouse hops like a miniature kangaroo on its large hind legs, crossing the bare ground between clumps of vegetation. It has a long tufted tail, which helps it keep its balance. Strangely, it has another adaptation which we saw last in a creature of the underground, the pocket gopher. This mouse has fur-lined cheek pockets too. These external pouches are used to carry the seeds on which it feeds.

Throughout the northern two-thirds of the plains and prairies, in areas of deep grass around sloughs and marshes, we occasionally see another attractive mouse built for covering the ground in great bounds, sometimes up to ten feet. This is the long-legged, extremely long-tailed—five inches or more—meadow jumping mouse. It is a seed eater, bright yellowish in color with a darker band down its back. As something different for a mouse, this one is a hibernator. Like many of the ground squirrels, it spends the long winter curled up in an underground nest, dead to the world.

The two-legged leaping gait and specialized development of the hind legs must enable many grassland creatures to escape their enemies. A larger animal so constructed is the kangaroo rat. (Presently we shall observe a still larger one, the jack rabbit.) Like the others, the kangaroo rat is fond of night foraging, and it will be seen frequently in sandy areas from Nebraska, south and west. Ten inches long, of a rich tawny color marked with white, and,

The ten-inch kangaroo rat—more than half that length is tail—is a solitary animal except at breeding time. It favors areas where the soil is loose or sandy enough to make tunneling easy, for it digs a labyrinth of passageways and chambers, often with a dozen or more entrances. Primarily a vegetarian, the kangaroo rat gathers seeds and other plant material and carefully cures them in the sun for several days before storing them underground. A single rat may lay up a bushel of food in its burrow!

A prairie rattler seeks relief from the hot midday sun in the shade of a badger burrow. Grassland snakes are most active during the morning and evening hours. Unable to regulate their body temperature by panting or sweating as mammals do, they must retreat underground during the hottest part of the day.

like other rodents of the dark, with large glistening eyes, this is one of the most striking and beautiful creatures of the grass.

Through their burrowing habits, small animals of the grasslands find a retreat from the heat of the day and from certain kinds of enemies. Of course, some predators, such as the badger, can dig them out; and others, such as the bull-snake, can go underground into their burrows.

Nibblers

Along wooded stream margins and wherever there is brushy cover in the grasslands, we see the common rabbit of North America, the cottontail. It nests in the grass and feeds on broad-leaved herbs, but it is truly an *edge* creature, for it also requires woody vegetation. It must have dense cover in winter, and its salvation is to hide rather than run away.

From the upper Mississippi River westward, the jack rabbit—more properly, a hare—is at home. If we divided the United States with an east-west line, the northern half of the grass country and semiarid brushlands would be the range of the white-tailed jack rabbit, a true northern animal that turns white in winter. The southern half belongs to the black-tailed jack, though there is a broad region of overlap between. Both jack rabbits live also in open lands far west.

White men will call the grassland hare a jack rabbit because its large, sensitive ears are like those of a jackass. It is rangy, with long hind legs, and it courses its ground in great leaps which, at intervals, take it above any surrounding cover for a clear view around. The large, maneuverable ears, bulging eyes, and great speed bespeak a creature with adaptations much like those of the antelope. But even in the open the jack rabbit can hide. In a sparse range of shortgrasses it can stop suddenly and disappear, its summer coat of grayish brown blending well with the dry vegetation. In its white winter phase the northern hare develops broad furry snowshoes on its hind feet. In deep snow it will dig a burrow for concealment.

The black-tailed jack rabbit of the South becomes amazingly abundant at times. But during the middle of the day we can walk through a heavily populated stand of bunch grass and low brush without ever seeing one. About four

Like the pronghorn, this white-tailed jack rabbit is built for survival by flight. Keen eyes and sensitive, swiveling ears give it an efficient early warning system; and the long, powerful hind legs let it dodge across the prairie at forty-five miles an hour, taking twenty-foot bounds and clearing five-foot-high obstacles with ease.

o'clock in the afternoon, tired of it all, we sit on a rock, wondering how the sun manages to stay so high and so hot for so long.

We move on. There beside a low bush of shadscale sits a jack rabbit licking its paws and grooming its head. Now look beyond: there is another. Where have they been? And here only thirty feet from us is a hare we had not noticed at all. Obviously the jack rabbits are coming out for a late-afternoon activity period. They do so quietly. All at once they are there, on every side.

These southern jacks eat a wide variety of vegetation. They browse most of the shrubs and eat many forbs and grasses. They feed commonly on the plentiful yellow-flowered broomweed, and they carefully prune away the spiny-tipped leaves of yucca. Studies of white-tailed jack rabbits in Kansas will show that their pellets contain many durable seeds of forbs and grasses, which are scattered over the range in excellent condition for germination. So, like the bison, the jack rabbit helps to manage its own range.

This animal, like other hares and rabbits, has a strange feeding habit. The plant materials that enter its digestive system are not fully broken down in one trip through. In blind pouches attached to the intestine, soft brown pellets are produced; these are excreted mainly during the jack rabbit's daylight hours of inactivity, at which time they are swallowed immediately for a second processing. These pellets are high in proteins, water-soluble vitamins, and other nutrients which are utilized as they are further digested by the microbial inhabitants of the hare's gut. Plant-feeding animals of many kinds depend on such minute living things to break down the cellulose and other components of their coarse plant foods. They commonly have long intestines for the lengthy digestive process. The jack rabbit gets more "mileage" by the twice-through process.

These hares of the grass and brush country do not burrow, but settle during the daytime in shallow depressions, or *forms*, dug in the ground surface either in the open

A black-tailed jack rabbit enjoys the shade of a yucca in the hot, arid grassland of the Southwest. Despite a host of enemies, jack rabbits flourish throughout the prairies. They are subject to local population explosions, during which their numbers increase to plague proportions.

93

or in thicker cover. The jack rabbit uses its grassland world principally at night. It is ideally adapted for looking, listening, and running.

Meat eaters at the top

Wherever we see buffalo, we also see wolves. They follow the buffalo herds and also scout bands of antelope, living from them as they may. The wolf of northern plains and prairies shows the kind of variability we would find in similar animals of the Arctic. Many of them are light gray or nearly white, with a pattern of darker markings on the back. A few are a darker gray shading to buff and cinnamon on the sides, more like the timber wolves on forest edges farther east. Some rare individuals of the plains wolf are a regal "blue" color, and their skins are held in veneration by Indians of the region.

Early and late, the slanting rays of the sun pick out the light-colored animals as brilliant white. Men who are to come with guns, traps, and poison will call them "white" wolves and will exterminate this handsome race before the year 1900.

Wolves commonly travel in packs of six to a dozen, but in spring we sometimes see a single individual curled in the sun near its den. The den is likely to be a remodeled badger hole in a sandy hillside, and fresh digging on the last snow of winter is likely to betray its presence.

The single wolf is probably one of a pair keeping watch over a litter of four or five while the other parent is off foraging. Sometimes several other wolves will loiter about the den, particularly after the pups are well enough along to be out sunning and romping on the slope. Perhaps they, too, are baby-sitting. The female travels many miles to recent remains of buffalo (they have to be recent or she would find only bare bones) and feeds heavily to replenish her milk. Also, she and the male bring meat to the den, chunks

The strikingly beautiful "white" race of plains wolf was still in existence when painter-naturalist John James Audubon visited the northern grasslands in 1843, but the animal was destined to be wiped out before the beginning of the twentieth century.

that have been swallowed and carried undigested in their stomachs, to be disgorged for the young. Later, as the youngsters grow, large pieces or entire dead animals may be brought in for the pups to chew and worry. Thus, they will be getting increasing amounts of the hair and bone that are the roughage in their diet.

Wolves are plentiful on the plains, as well they may be. We need not doubt that their numbers are adjusted to the abundant hoofed-animal food supply.

We have noted a smaller wolflike creature, the coyote, also to be common in the grassland. It takes the leavings around carcasses fed upon by the plains wolf, but its own hunting is largely for lesser prey, such as rodents, rabbits, hares, and insects. In season it feeds well on all the fruits of the range.

Well after sundown, but while clouds of the western horizon still glow with mauve and red, these little dogs of the grass country assemble on some knoll or crest and break forth in their first song of evening—a riot of yipping, yap-

Although the gray wolf has virtually vanished from nearly all the grasslands, its smaller and more adaptable relative, the coyote, still holds out in many areas against poisoning and other "predator-control" efforts. Indeed, during the past twenty years the coyote has increased its range and numbers in forested lands of eastern states.

ping, and ki-yiing. We would guess there were twenty at least if we were not close enough to count only five.

Later in the night we are likely to hear the deeper ringing call of a wolf, and it too may set off a chorus of wild dog music. This time there is more throat and power, heavy with basso and contralto. There is no doubt that the ruler of the plains is being heard.

That rule may well be contested in the grassy badlands of the upper Missouri River. For there with luck we can see another creature, whose pelt is so light a shade of sun-bleached gray that it will be called the great white bear. It is a huge and powerful grizzly that, from its racial infancy, has never had to turn aside for man or beast. The Indian brave of this early day gains great honor by killing a white bear with his crude bow and arrow and lance. Trapper-explorers of the 1800s will give this animal a wide berth, when it is seen in time.

The badlands grizzly is another wild species that will be extinct by the beginning of the twentieth century. In its kinship the bear is a carnivore, but, like man, it eats anything and everything. Opportunity presenting, it feeds on animals large and small, as well as on insects, roots, berries,

Audubon was still able to observe and paint the badlands grizzly bear when he journeyed up the Missouri River to Montana and North Dakota in 1843. Before the turn of the century, this distinctive race of grizzlies was wiped out in the path of the settlers' steady westward push.

and oak mast in the edge lands. It has great sicklelike claws for digging and slashing, long canine teeth for seizing, and blunt molars for crushing. The grizzly does not hibernate but in winter retires to a cave or the narrow bottom of a leaf-clogged gully where it can roll up protected by its thick layer of back fat and be drifted over by the snow. It remains inactive until spring.

Small hunters

One could not watch the grassland creatures for long without seeing that the profusion of specialist plant feeders is complemented by a similar variety of flesh-eating animals. Each inhabitant of the grasslands has its own design for living, by which it fits a particular *niche* in its life community.

We have already noted how well the badger is suited to its job of digging out ground squirrels. In this environment of the grassland it is the largest member of the weasel family. Another of the weasel kin, the black-footed ferret, also lives on burrowing rodents, but it has solved the supply problem in quite a different way.

The black-footed ferret is creamy brown above and lighter below, with a dark mask across the eyes. It is slender and agile, the right size and shape to "break and enter" prairie-dog burrows. And that is how it lives. It inhabits prairie-dog towns and appears to have every advantage for feeding on these abundant and easily found rodents.

With such easy living, why are the grasslands not overrun with ferrets? It is true that this small carnivore is not plentiful even in these early times. Much later, biologists will discover that many animals, and particularly the meat eaters, have various kinds of built-in social intolerances that prevent excessive population build-ups. Possibly this is true of the ferret. It is not certain that anyone can ever find out for sure, since this small hunter will nearly disappear when the grasslands are converted to livestock range and grainfields and men "control" the prairie dog with poison. By

The black-footed ferret, shown here in an Audubon painting, is dependent upon the prairie-dog town for both shelter and food. Man's wholesale destruction of the prairie dog has had the side effect of so reducing the black-footed ferret population that this handsome weasel is now the rarest mammal in all of North America.

the middle of the twentieth century the ferret will be the rarest mammal in North America.

Rodents of the night have many troubles, as we can witness by watching early and late in the vicinity of rocky ledges, gullies, and other rough places. There we frequently notice a slender, short-legged creature, with long neck and arched back, that stops sometimes to wave its small whiskered head from side to side, testing the air. It slips in and out of mouseholes, a specialist obviously! The long-tailed weasel is a master hunter of the smallest rodents, yet capable of handling prey the size of cottontails.

The weasels have still other relatives in the prairies and plains of central North America, for when moonlight favors we can sometimes see the black and white pattern of the little spotted skunk as this animal leaves its den in a thicket of coralberry or streamside willows. It noses busily in the ground litter for beetles, crickets, and other insects, and it is adept at finding a nest of young mice.

The larger striped skunk is more plentiful, and at dusk in early summer it is frequently afield leading its young on a night's hunt. On a crisp morning in the fall these skunks will

be found plucking chilled grasshoppers from the vegetation or digging beetle larvae out of the sod. They will fatten well and then hole up for a long winter in a grass-lined den. Like the bear, the skunk does not hibernate. During the long sleep its temperature and pulse rate are at usual levels, and any disturbance will rouse the animal quickly. As we might expect, northern skunks have a longer period of inactivity, while those in the South hole up only during severe weather.

In western grasslands, over a broad range from north to south, we commonly encounter another of the doglike predators related to the wolf and the coyote. This is the dainty and graceful kit fox. As befits a species of the sun-drenched high plains, it is pale buff in color. Though smaller than other foxes, it is amazingly fast as it bounds lightly over the low vegetation, balanced by its thick plumelike tail. The kit, or swift, fox feeds on rodents, rabbits, and hares. By the early part of the twentieth century it will be a rare animal, faring poorly amid the general poisoning of rodents and predators that will become a widespread practice in the western states.

Plumed tails waving, a mother striped skunk and her brood journey forth in quest of grasshoppers, grubs, and small rodents. The animals' well-known chemical defense system keeps most would-be predators at a respectful distance. The great horned owl is an exception, and occasionally one of these big nocturnal birds will be found reeking from a recent spraying.

With a staccato rattling of quills
and an almost turkeylike
gobbling, two sharp-tailed
grouse cocks try to outdo each
other in their colorful
springtime courtship ritual. . . .

Boomers of the spring

One of the first creatures we saw on our grand tour was the
heath hen of the coastal barrens. Other prairie grouse are
conspicuous as we go from one part of the grasslands to
another. The one common to a great region from Canada
to central Texas and Ohio is to be known as the greater
prairie chicken. Westward, in the Texas panhandle, is a high-
plains subspecies, the lesser prairie chicken. Still a third,
a smaller and darker race that lives on the Texas coastal
plain, will be named Attwater's prairie chicken.

As we might expect, these birds of the grasslands will disappear as the native prairie is broken up for agriculture.
By the middle of the twentieth century there will be only

102

remnant populations here and there, a situation we can hardly conceive amid the abundance we see in the late 1400s.

In a broad region on each side of the Canadian line, we have seen large numbers—sometimes several hundred in a fall flock—of a bird so similar to the prairie chicken that we might easily have mistaken it for one. This one has a pointed tail and thereby gets its name: sharp-tailed grouse. Actually, the sharptail is more a bird of brushy edges, but finding it scattered far and wide over northern prairies is not at all inconsistent. For the thick stands of wolfberry and silverberry that are so common on the prairie, as well as the stream-bottom woodlands and the thickets of chokecherry, "lemonade" sumac, and other shrubs that mark the steep breaks of glacial deposits—these in effect create brushy edges everywhere. They seem to make the open grassland a favorable and productive range for the sharptail.

All of the prairie grouse are found, like the heath hen, on their booming grounds in early spring. Amid the last snowfalls of March and April the males will gather on some open hillside at dawn. They establish their courting territories and dance and strut and mate as countless generations of chickens have done for millions of years.

Somewhere in thick grasses the hen makes her nest and lays her eggs, which are well colored for concealment, olive to buff, lightly sprinkled and dotted with brown. Soon after

... Pattering their feet, pointing spread tails straight up, inflating air sacs of the neck, lunging and feinting at each other, the cocks display in the age-old pattern of the dancing ground.

hatching, the brood leaves the nest—a dozen tiny balls of fluff that follow the hen and feed avidly on a starter diet of high-protein insects she finds for them. In late mornings we can watch them dusting on a sunny hillside in the loose soil of a gopher digging. Often the head of the mother is held high, on the alert for marauders overhead.

Habits of the prairie chicken and sharptail are so nearly

alike that they may be found performing on the same booming ground, and occasionally they interbreed. Both feed on the fleshy fruits of the prairie, and their droppings scatter the pits to sprout and grow wherever the situation is right. They likewise consume the abundance of seeds and grain produced by forbs and grasses. During winter, when snow is deep, the flocks move into young woodlands to eat the buds of aspen and other acceptable kinds of trees and shrubs.

In spring, on a side trip westward into the brushy ranges of Wyoming, we shall find the largest grouse of the continent, the sage grouse. It is evident that this is a bird of the open spaces, for its mating display is much like that of the prairie chicken, the sharptail, and other grassland

Several hundred sage grouse cocks may gather together on a northern prairie booming ground covering an area perhaps two hundred yards wide and half a mile long.

grouse of the world. It establishes dancing areas, where the territorial ritual of the six-pound cock is truly spectacular. His huge air sacs nearly drag the ground as he parades through a fantastic display in the gray light of dawn. Few of these birds are seen east of Montana and Wyoming. They thrive best amid the sage-clad hills and plains of the Great Basin.

105

Those of a feather

Spring on the prairie is a time when one must wade and slosh across endless mushy sods and flats of standing water. It is the green-up period, and great swarms of bird life are moving northward over the land. A medley of cries, calls, and wing beatings disturbs the air by day and night.

Long before all the snows of March have melted from northern slopes, the male horned lark's jingling can be heard from somewhere high above. Then we see him plunging earthward to certain destruction. No, he breaks and touches lightly down, on the run. Nearby a female is lining, with fibers, a scooped-out hollow among the rootstocks.

On bright warm days our ears throb with the clear bell tones of the most characteristic bird of the grasslands. Somewhere west of Lake Michigan, the cheering whistle of meadowlarks, so familiar farther east, changes its character and becomes a throaty ringing melody. Our ear tells us that we have left the domain of the eastern meadowlark and are now hearing another species, the western meadowlark. We could not tell the difference simply by seeing them. The bird that rides a swaying stalk of last year's rosinweed could be either kind.

In a later century the schoolchildren of Kansas will vote for the western meadowlark as their state bird. In tribute to this universal favorite, the western meadowlark will also be the state bird of Montana, Nebraska, North Dakota, Oregon, and Wyoming.

In June and July on eastern prairies, male dickcissels call from every patch of deep grass and forbs. There also, the bubbling outburst of the male bobolink pours forth as he glides on set wings over the hidden nest where his brown-streaked mate incubates her clutch. Realistically, this is not a song of joy: it is warning to other male bobolinks that a claim has been established and this is a piece of the prairie that is not to be invaded.

This is indeed why all the male birds sing. It is what makes it possible for us to sit on a glacial boulder, close our eyes, and identify the bird life in a great circle around us.

A bird we have seen frequently on the open lands is one that follows the buffalo, as later it will follow the white man's cattle and earn the name of cowbird. It is somewhat the color of a buffalo; the male is black with a brown head and neck, the female a nondescript gray.

YELLOW-HEADED BLACKBIRD

Cowbirds feed—oftentimes with red-winged blackbirds—at the heels of the buffalo, picking up insects stirred by the passing hoofs. They perch on the backs of the big animals, which pay no attention, and pluck ticks or insects. One might expect that this bison bird would make its nest of wool, but no such thing. It does not make any kind of nest. The female lays her egg in the nest of another bird, and the foster parents raise the strong, greedy young cowbird and often lose their own offspring! In other words, the cowbird is a nesting parasite.

Birds everywhere

Certain kinds of birds are so common and widespread over the prairies and plains that we expect them wherever we go. One that is seldom out of sight or sound is the killdeer. Its unmistakable call is heard frequently at night. Two other shore birds are found widely in their preferred grassland habitats: the upland plover in tallgrass and mixed-grass prairies and the long-billed curlew on the high plains. Both have loud musical calls. Red-winged blackbirds are before us in nearly all our travels, centering their activity near tall vegetation in low ground and wet edges. In the North they are replaced or joined locally by the colorful yellow-headed blackbirds.

On the northern prairie there are other kinds of slender and long-legged wading birds that nest commonly around the water holes—especially the marbled godwit and willet. During spring and fall migrations we unexpectedly see small needle-billed shore birds bobbing and darting on the open water of marshes and ponds. They whirl in endless gyrations, dabbling in the water for mosquito larvae and other minute living things. These tiny feathered sprites are phalaropes. The grayish northern phalarope is a transient in the grasslands, stopping on its way to and from its nesting ground far to the north and its winter home far south. The more brightly colored Wilson's phalarope nests in well-watered prairies and then migrates to South America.

In these same wet areas in the prairies and plains certain songbirds always live among the sedges, whitetop, and slough grass. They are the Nelson's sharp-tailed sparrow, Le Conte's sparrow, and savannah sparrow. We come to know them by their distinctive songs, which have buzzing insectlike qualities. This is true also of the grasshopper sparrow, so common in the mixed-grass uplands. At this

BOBOLINK

WADERS OF THE GRASSLANDS

Of the great world-wide order of wading or shore birds, most have breeding grounds in the Arctic and each spring and fall pass high over the central grasslands in their great migration flocks. But several species of waders are summer residents of the prairies and plains, nesting in the grass and weeds and feeding in the potholes and wet meadows. Then, with the coming of autumn, they again join the great hosts of migrants for the general movement southward.

Some of the waders winter along the Gulf and south along both coasts of Mexico. Others travel far down across the equator to the pampas of South America, where another spring is in progress. There they feed and fatten until the shortening days of February and March impel them again to follow the sun northward to their breeding grounds.

The upland plover (top) *conceals its nest in a heavy clump of grass on the open prairie. The marbled godwit* (bottom), *second in size only to the long-billed curlew among the wading birds, seeks the moist pothole country of the northern grasslands.*

The largest, best publicized, and most imperiled of our native water birds, the stately whooping crane once bred throughout the northern prairies and wintered along the Gulf Coast from Florida to Mexico. Today the whooper teeters at the very brink of extinction. The total wild population is about four dozen, and the only remaining breeding range is in the Northwest Territories of Canada.

higher level in the drainage, the tinkling notes of Baird's sparrow sound from hillsides green with blue grama, thread-leaf sedge, and needlegrass.

Some of the small birds that occur widely in the plains extend eastward into the mixed-grass prairie, where they are largely restricted to drier, sparsely grassed areas. Examples are the chestnut-collared and McCown's longspurs, Sprague's pipit, and the horned lark. We have noted that the lark bunting, a black bird with large white wing patches, flushes most frequently from sites of disturbed soil or heavy grazing.

It is worth reflecting on the fact that a common marking of small grassland birds is a white border on the tail. This is true of longspurs, pipits, and the horned lark, meadowlark, and vesper sparrow. And doesn't it seem remarkable that the pattern of yellow and black on the breast of the male dickcissel is so much like that of the meadowlark? Also, listen to the peculiar ticking sequences in the songs of the grasshopper sparrow and horned lark, and notice how similar they are. How is it that the grassland habitat tends to mold its creatures into certain patterns for their welfare and survival? If we could have watched this happen through the ages, we might understand it better.

The two largest birds in North America—the whooping crane and the trumpeter swan—nest in the larger marshes of the grassland. Both are gleaming white and carry their long necks extended. Both have clarion calls that resound for miles across the hills. Their orderly V formations and echelons show brightly against the sky as they move in flocks of a few dozen, early and late in the season. They are highly territorial, scattering out widely for their nesting, with individual pairs laying claim to hundreds of acres of marsh and shoreline.

These two great birds are easily distinguished from afar. The trumpeter is totally white, and the whooping crane has black flight feathers in its wings. By the early twentieth century their grassland populations will be gone. The trumpeter swan will be saved from extinction by a few dozen pairs that maintain themselves in the Yellowstone country and northward. These will increase under careful protection. By the 1960s less than four dozen whoopers will be left. They will have an undisturbed nesting retreat in the wild muskegs of the Northwest Territories in Canada and a wintering ground at Aransas National Wildlife Refuge on the Texas coast.

The trumpeter swan is another victim of man's short-sightedness and greed. Thousands of the birds were slaughtered during the nineteenth century by private and commercial hunters. A few survived in a remote area of the Yellowstone region, and these formed a nucleus population which has built up steadily under effective protection in recent years.

The plains and prairies that we see so vibrant with life in spring and summer will be a different place in winter. Then the vast reaches of windswept white will appear desolate and deserted except where pronghorns or the great buffalo herds pass. The small birds of winter will be seed eaters which feed on the standing heads of forbs and grasses. Many, like the snow bunting and Lapland longspur, move down from far-northern nesting areas to winter on the plains. In general the grassland community is reduced and simplified in winter. The great host of insect life and cold-blooded animals of all types have disappeared or dug in below frostline. In northern regions many of the mammals are sleeping out the season, and most of the breeding birds are in summer resorts far to the south.

Birds of passage

The animals that "belong" and have greatest influence in the grass country are those that live and breed here. But the prairies and plains also are an important seasonal habitat for the millions of migrant birds that pass through early and late as they follow warm weather north and then retreat again to lower latitudes. The movement southward begins as a flocking and shifting in midsummer and builds to a sky-filling crescendo as feathered multitudes pour down from the Arctic in autumn.

The traverse of the plains includes birds of every habit, including ground species, brushland species, clouds of swallows, marsh birds such as rails, coots, and grebes, as well as herons, hawks, owls, diving ducks, dabbling ducks, geese, whistling swans, sandhill cranes, and a wide variety of sandpipers and other shore birds.

Several kinds of migrant shore birds are of particular interest because of their abundance, their habits, and what will happen to them in centuries to come. A strikingly beautiful species—with a black belly, brilliant white markings,

The northern prairie is silent and somber during the long winter. The bison and pronghorn are still active, but most of the birds have long since departed for the South and many of the small mammals have retired to their burrows.

115

The golden plover is a springtime visitor to the prairies as it moves from Argentina to its Arctic breeding grounds. On the return trip southward in the fall, this robin-sized bird will make a nonstop 2400-mile flight across the Atlantic from Labrador to Brazil.

and a back flecked richly with yellow—is the golden plover. From its winter home in the Argentine grasslands, it comes north through Texas and the prairies west of the Mississippi River in March and April. We sometimes see flats or depressions blanketed with thousands of golden plovers busily prying into the sod for the first emerging insects of spring. It is a season of relative scarcity, and they cover great areas in their foraging.

The plovers feed northward to the parklands of Canada, then move on to their breeding grounds in the western Arctic. We will see few of them again this year, for their fall movement is mainly to the southeast for a staging on the coast of Labrador and Nova Scotia. From there the flight is over the ocean to the coast of Brazil, and then on south to the Argentine pampas.

This bird is swift of wing, unwary, and a dainty morsel. Bird hunters will slaughter it mercilessly on the prairies in spring, on the northeast coast in late summer, and again in winter in South America. After 1875 the big flocks will be gone. The plover with gold on its back will become a rarity. Fortunately, growing protection will rescue it in time and permit it to survive in small numbers.

The fate of the dough bird

In these early days, Indians of the Texas coast mark the progress of their year by familiar seasonal events. In particular they know that spring arrives with the curlews. From somewhere south great flocks that must total millions sail in to landings on the sacahuiste flats. There they rest and feed before moving on.

The Eskimo curlew is a size smaller than that familiar high-plains nester, the long-billed curlew. It is vastly more abundant, and it is bound for the arctic coastlines. On the way it takes its leisure in the grassland, moving north with the blooming of the willows. Even in spring, it lives well on this productive land.

From afar, we learn to recognize a massed flight of Eskimo curlews. Commonly it forms a great wedge with sides eddying out into smokelike wisps and trailing streamers. Swirling and swooping, towering and twisting, the airborne

116

avalanche sweeps across the sky, and the voice of the throng speaks to us in a subdued undertone of mellow whistles. Other times the curlew call rings loud and clear as a wandering dozen of the migrants pass us by day or night.

Over hundreds of acres we watch feeding flocks probing the sod for grasshopper egg cases carefully buried last fall by females now long dead. The curlews share grubs, beetles, and all manner of worms and insects of the dry uplands with the golden and black-bellied plovers, meadowlarks, and others.

In its migration path from the Arctic, the Eskimo curlew continues to follow the golden plover southeast to Labrador. There the hordes will fatten on late-summer crops of berries, and then they, too, will disappear over the misty waters of the Atlantic Ocean on a nonstop flight to the Brazilian coast.

Of all the shore birds, this one will be most easily shot in great numbers—in three seasons of the year, like the plovers. In spring on the American prairies, shooters will fill their buckboards with curlews and load the game markets with cheap meat. The "sport" will often be so good that great numbers of birds will be left on the ground. Fall shooting on the northeast coast will be known around the world. There hunters will call the Eskimo curlew a "dough bird" because, pound-heavy and layered with fat, it will feel like dough when held in the hand. During northern winters, there will be more shooting on the South American range.

It is strange that a bird so successful in the early wilderness will disappear quickly before the guns of a later day. By 1900 only stragglers will be left, and by 1960 reports of sightings will be years apart. This will be the fate of a wild creature that was tender eating and had no fear of man.

Many times we have remarked on the spectacular twice-a-year movement of waterfowl in this central flyway of the continent. One of the great spectacles of spring is the thousands of many species courting, pairing, chasing, and displaying as they progress toward their nesting places in the pothole country or farther north to the parklands, open tundra, lakes, and winding rivers. After the nesting and rearing there is a general flocking—first of drakes, then a mixture of old and young—on the marshes and lakes of the grasslands.

How did the Eskimo curlews, often traveling at night and over long stretches of featureless ocean, navigate the eight thousand miles that separated their winter home in the South American pampas and their summer breeding grounds in the Canadian Arctic? For scientists who study animal behavior, bird navigation is among the most tantalizing of Nature's riddles. Visual landmarks and the positions of the sun and stars probably play a part; birds may also possess special senses that respond to the earth's rotation and magnetic field.

BREEDING AREA

WINTERING AREA

As late as the 1880s, the Eskimo curlew (shown here in an Audubon painting) moved northward over the prairies in huge flights numbering millions of birds. Gunners indulged in the dubious sport of bringing down a dozen or more curlews with a single blast from a shotgun; commercial hunters shipped them by the ton to the ready markets in the East. The supply seemed inexhaustible. Then, within a single decade, the Eskimo curlew population dwindled rapidly. In 1890 the last curlew was sighted in Indiana. In 1899, the last Wisconsin sighting was made, until a lone male was seen in 1912. The bird disappeared from Kansas in 1902. A single bird was shot in western Nebraska in 1915. Scattered sightings were made during the 1920s, but during the 1930s only a single bird, shot in Newfoundland, was reported. That was the last of the Eskimo curlews until 1945, when a sighting, again of a single bird, was made over Galveston Island, Texas. Then, in 1959, the curlew began what seemed like a possible rally. From that year through 1964, at least one and sometimes two of the birds were reported each year, mostly over Galveston Island. But 1965 and 1966 passed with no sightings whatever. Has the Eskimo curlew finally lost its long struggle against extinction? No one can say for sure, but it now seems appropriate to list the bird as "missing in action—presumed dead."

Sky patrol

Among the most conspicuous and interesting birds of the grasslands are those that hunt for a living, the feathered predators. Now they are at their best, their maximum numbers, before guns of the nineteenth and twentieth centuries bring about their widespread destruction. Every day these birds have something new to show us, as each in its own way courses the open swards for its particular prey.

No one could miss the golden eagle as it swoops on set pinions to a prairie-dog colony and then flashes at low level across the ground, sending the startled rodents shrieking into their holes. An unwary animal is likely to be snatched aloft and carried to a feeding perch on some nearby rocky outcrop. Frequently the eagle's dash may be rewarded with an eight-pound jack rabbit, antelope kid, rattlesnake, or sage grouse.

The eagle we watch was hatched in a stick nest on the shelf of some canyon wall in mountains to the west. This individual is totally dark brown with golden hackles on its head, and so we know it is an adult, at least four years old. In younger birds the underwing has a white area, and the base of the tail is grayish white. Those tail feathers are in demand as headdress materials among Indians of the plains.

Handily surpassing the eagle in speed, dash, and "class" is the prairie falcon, near relative of the peregrine falcon so popular as a trained hunting bird among European royalty in the Middle Ages. The prairie falcon has pointed wings (this is true of all falcons), a facial marking like a black mustache, and heavy feet. It is a courser of the airways, one of the fastest birds on the continent. It lives mainly on feathered prey taken in full flight.

One could never tire of watching and marveling at the control and easy power of this bird as it idles along, seemingly with all the world to choose from. Then suddenly its action changes. Diving down from the blue in a blaze of speed, it bludgeons a duck, grouse, or dove out of the air with a hammer blow from its knuckled foot. A puff of feathers, a thud, and the prey goes hurtling down, but not far. The agile falcon swoops, takes it delicately in a taloned foot, and sails away.

A smaller falcon, lacking the speed, but of equal style and beauty, is the plentiful little sparrow hawk. This one perches on a bush or tree, surveying neighboring meadows

Wings spreading a full seven feet, a golden eagle patrols the prairie sky, its keen eyes watching for the telltale movement of a jack rabbit or a prairie dog.

120

for the grasshoppers, small birds, and occasional mice on which it feeds. We find that watching hawks in the clear air of the grasslands sometimes poses problems of size and distance. A dark bird against the light may be a sparrow hawk at a hundred yards or a prairie falcon at a quarter-mile. Then the bird stops and hovers in one spot on beating wings—it is a sparrow hawk.

The sparrow hawk pays no attention to a long-winged white-rumped harrier, the marsh hawk, which quarters in leisurely butterflylike flight a few feet above the tallgrass margins. This weak-legged bird takes small prey, prairie voles, ground squirrels, snakes, frogs, and young birds. It favors low ground and often nests on a muskrat house.

In similar habitat of the tallgrass prairie, we find an owl quite like the marsh hawk in hunting and nesting habits. Its food is largely mice. The short-eared owls, light buff in color and long of wing, cruise lightly above the grasses before sunrise and in the cool of evening. On overcast days they may be abroad at any time. They shift southward in winter, and sometimes a dozen of them will habitually roost together in the tangled vegetation of a stream bottom.

The birds of prey that we see most frequently on the grassland are big broad-winged soaring hawks. These will also be known as buzzard hawks, or buteos. The soaring hawks are feeders on small animals, mice, rats, ground squirrels, rabbits, lizards, and the like. The red-tailed hawk is one of the largest and commonest of this group. Its color patterns can be quite confusing in the field. They vary from light to dark, and some birds do not even have a red tail. However, typical redtails are easy to recognize. As we watch one wheeling on the air currents at a great height, tipping and turning, the sun picks up the rich rufous-red of its upper tail surface. Then, we hear faintly its rasping cry. Like other buzzard hawks, the redtail nests in timbered border country on a platform of sticks high in the fork of a tree.

In spring an observer of the grasslands is likely to see one of the most impressive of all hawk migrations. It is the northward movement of large milling flocks (hundreds or even thousands) of a hawk with a dark band across its throat. White men will name it for a famous student of birds and call it Swainson's hawk.

This one winters in Mexico, flying north to nest in timber belts of the plains. It is adept at plucking flying insects out of the air with a taloned foot. In fact, the reason for the

An expert rider of air currents, the red-tailed hawk, with a wingspan of about four feet, feeds mainly on rabbits and such rodents as mice and ground squirrels.

curious gyrations of many flocks of Swainson's hawks is that the birds chase down and feed on swarms of high-flying grasshoppers. Insects are a main food of this particular buteo.

A beautiful and distinctive member of this great group of hawks lives far to the south on the coastal plain of Texas. It is recognized easily by its underparts, rump, and tail of shining white. It will be known as Sennet's white-tailed hawk; and its favorite nesting site in these southern savannahs is in the top of a thorny blackbrush, eight or ten feet above the ground.

Feathered to the toes

Swainson's hawk, distinguished by its dark breast band, is about the size of the redtail but has more pointed wings. This summer resident of the grasslands winters in Mexico and then moves north in spectacular flocks in spring.

In our discussion of grassland birds of prey, it seems fitting to find a place of prominence for the large and handsomely marked roughlegs—so called because their legs are feathered, like those of the eagle, down to the toes.

Rough-legged hawks occur in a wide variety of striking patterns of buff and brown, some so dark that they look black against the sky. They are long-winged and completely at home soaring and circling high above the earth on the

changing air currents of a summer day. These birds are among the best of mousehawks, for their small feet and talons are unmistakably fitted for handling small prey. Of course, they include prairie dogs, rabbits, and an occasional hare in their menu.

The American rough-legged hawk breeds in the Far North and winters on the prairies and plains. Frequently in flight it stops and hovers in one spot, exactly like the elegant little sparrow hawk. Over our entire region in the cold season these roughlegs are often seen sitting conspicuously on old cottonwood stubs in the river bottoms or other high trees in the edge country. They sun themselves and watch with their telescopic eyes for any movement on the grassland. In its light phases this hawk commonly has a conspicuous pattern, dark brown on the belly, the angle of the wing, and the banded end of the tail. The rump is light like that of the marsh hawk.

The largest and certainly one of the most beautiful hawks we shall see is another roughleg, the ferruginous hawk. Sci-

The rough-legged hawk displays the specialized equipment of the prairie's feathered predators: broad wings and fan-shaped tail for long periods of almost effortless soaring; prominent eyes, eight times keener than those of man; needle-sharp talons and a powerful curved beak.

entists will call this one *Buteo regalis*, and it is indeed a regal bird. It is a year-round resident of the grass country, nesting to the northern limits in timbered edges, on cliff-sides, and occasionally on the ground. Northern breeders withdraw to the southern half of this range in winter.

When we see this striking buteo, we are not likely to mistake it for any other hawk. The adult light-phase bird stands out in immaculate buffy white against the blue of the sky. In the flight feathers near the end of the wing is a conspicuous light spot, or lens. The darker reddish legs form a V as they come together beneath the tail.

The first-year young of ferruginous hawks and other roughlegs are darker in overall coloration. And the occurrence of many color phases ensures that we shall see every kind of pattern between the light and dark extremes. This adds endless interest to our observations of these birds, for one gets the feeling that Nature let herself go on the rough-legs and did a custom job of design.

Society and survival

As travelers in the grassland we have commonly seen single animals, or sometimes breeding pairs. In the warm season we have also watched family groups in which the relationships of parents to offspring are fairly evident. And our observations of the buffalo herds and prairie-dog towns have shown us clearly that there are larger social gatherings, which appear to be well organized. Certain individuals in a colony or herd are aggressive and dominant; usually they have their way in the selection of mates and homesites. Others, less capable, may be underprivileged and far down the social order. But each individual has its position in the local society. By knowing the "rules," it can get along and largely avoid destructive conflict with its own kind. Thus the behavior patterns of a species, quite as much as its physical characteristics, influence its ability to survive.

A Richardson's ground squirrel squats beside its burrow, alert for the shadow of a swooping hawk or the movement of a weasel through the grass. Predator or prey, large or small, social or solitary, each creature of the prairie occupies its own special niche in the dynamic grassland community.

The Wild

Community

As we have seen, grasslands are the home and habitat of a great variety of living things. And it is becoming evident that Nature did not just throw together here a by-chance assembly of plants and animals to take up space. Each species of this wild *community* has a job to do; it occupies a certain niche in the pattern of life. It developed its specialty through ages of geological time, by a coldly impartial process of trial and error. This is a world of time-proven order. By now we may properly suspect that in this world of the wild the only thing disorderly is that which we do not yet understand!

By its very nature, a community is flexible and adaptable, and for good reasons. There have been many changes in the land over which we have traveled. Some important ones occurred since the last glacial period. For example, a few thousand years ago, at a time of higher rainfall, trees were much more plentiful in the central and northern prairies. The relatively arid climates, most suitable for grass, probably had shifted southward. Associations of plants and animals shifted also, and no doubt many species were lost in the process.

To maintain its place in the community, a species must be successful in meeting competition and in using the food

and other resources of the environment. But what if it were too successful? That would not work, because such a species would destroy the things on which it depended. Obviously no fine point of structure or habit has escaped the sifting and selecting of the evolutionary process.

The study of communities of living things and their relationships with each other and with their surroundings is a life science called *ecology*. Ecologists are learning much that is important to all of us. The more we know about the operation of the natural world, the better we can manage the plants and animals we must have to live. In the end, man must be a coexisting part of his own world-wide community if he is to keep on using it, indeed if he is to survive in it at all.

Let us look more deeply within this life association of the grassland as it was in primitive times. We shall be concerned with not only what went on but also how and why.

Inside the green leaf

The land of turf, "weeds," bunch grasses, and drought-resistant shrubs is a realm of sunshine. The energy originating in the sun's atomic fire pot makes all life possible.

The leaves of every green plant are spread to catch solar radiation and use it as the energy basis for the chemistry of life. On a single acre of prairie the total exposed leaf surface is from five to ten acres! The green substance in which the key reaction, *photosynthesis*, takes place is called *chlorophyll*.

In the chlorophyll of leaves, water and minerals from the soil are brought together with carbon dioxide from the air. Elements from these compounds are combined chemically through a great tying up of energy. The process forms basic nutrients, sugars and starches, that are further changed and complicated by the addition of nitrogen to form proteins.

Nitrogen also comes from the air. It is made available by specialist organisms, nitrogen-fixing bacteria, which live

The prairie's green plants, such as the foxtail barley shown here, collectively form a great chemical factory that uses the energy of the sun to convert inorganic raw materials into foodstuffs.

128

in root nodules of plants belonging to the pea family. These bacteria release soluble nitrates that are taken up with water by the exploring rootlets of grasses and other herbs.

This is the way plants are nourished, and the result is growth. The formation of living substances—complex organic compounds—is the process that supports all kinds of life. It takes place mainly in the warm season of the year and depends heavily on the amount of available moisture and other environmental factors.

So we can say that green plants are the basic manufacturing units of the life community. They take in great quantities of raw materials—soluble compounds from the breakdown of parent minerals of the soil, and an abundance of reprocessed organic residues from living things. The growth of plants is the *primary production* in this realm of life. Plants are the first and original *producers*, and the energy they tie up is transferred from one kind of organism to another as each feeds and is fed upon according to its place in the community.

The story of the interrelations of living things is largely one of how basic nourishment is passed around and circulated in the *ecosystem*—the community of plants and animals together with the rest of the environment, including soil, site, and water. For some purposes we should talk about ecosystems rather than just communities, because they present a broader view of the interrelationships of living things.

Hopping consumers

There are numerous kinds of animals that make direct use of the living tissues of plants. In fact, these vegetarians are the most abundant creatures of any community, and it is realistic to regard them as *primary consumers*. We cannot walk very far through the grasslands without getting the feel of what is going on. In summer a swarm of grasshoppers click away on short jerky flights in front of us.

Grasshoppers and their relatives are among the most plentiful and influential animals of this great biome. In each state of the northern Great Plains there are more than a hundred kinds of grasshoppers. In a later century, the economic entomologists will be concerned about this, because grasshoppers are ideally adapted to feeding on cultivated crops. Over thousands of years the swarms of locusts, or short-

Lambert crazyweed blooms conspicuously on mixed prairies in late spring and early summer. This perennial is one of several legumes commonly called "loco." It is toxic to some creatures, particularly horses, cattle, sheep, and goats. Besides slowly poisoning the animals that feed on it, it also turns them into crazyweed addicts.

horned grasshoppers, on semiarid lands have periodically brought destruction to growing grain and famine to many peoples.

Although there are many species of grasshoppers, a few are most widespread and abundant. Nearly everywhere in the prairies and plains we shall find the two-striped, the red-legged, and the lesser migratory grasshoppers. The differential grasshopper is found from South Dakota south, and widely across the North one of the most common species is the clear-winged grasshopper. If one wanted to devote his life to it, he could become a specialist on this group of insects and always have plenty to do.

Of the great variety of grasshoppers in different regions, about half actually eat grasses. Likewise, about half live on other broad-leaved herbs, or forbs, of the grasslands. Thus, practically the entire vegetation is being used and, in some degree, turned into animal form by these nearly universally distributed insects. Of course, the extent to which this happens in a particular year can vary widely. When grasshoppers are abundant, there might be thirty of them to the square yard. At this density the population on two acres could consume in a season as much forage as a buffalo.

Grasshoppers are among the most important of the grassland's primary consumers. They are divided into two great families: the longhorns, such as the one clinging to the grass leaf above, and the shorthorns, such as the one perched atop the buffalo bur at the left. Most of the destructive pest species, including the infamous locusts, come from the ranks of the shorthorn grasshoppers.

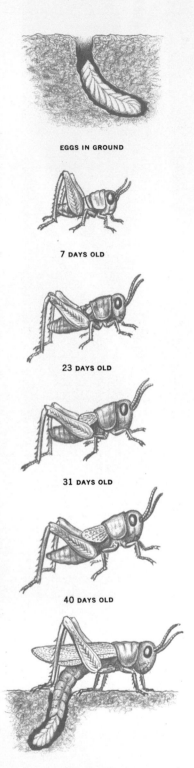

EGGS IN GROUND

7 DAYS OLD

23 DAYS OLD

31 DAYS OLD

40 DAYS OLD

FULL-GROWN

Unlike insects that pass through a definite larval stage, grasshoppers emerge from the egg as nymphs—tiny creatures that closely resemble the adult in form, differing from it primarily in their incompletely developed wings and their inability to carry out reproductive functions.

Ordinarily, grasshoppers are not this numerous, because they have high loss rates; that is, many of them die before they reach adulthood. In late fall the females deposit their water-resistant egg cases in the ground: an average laying for all species would be about two hundred eggs. All the adults of the population die. Of the total eggs laid, roughly a fifth are destroyed by plovers, curlews, and other predators. After the spring hatch, about sixty percent of the young grasshoppers are lost in early stages. And from then on the older *nymphs*, or immature hoppers, and the adults are further thinned out by predators, diseases, and parasites before egg-laying time. When the grasshopper population is the same from one year to the next, only one pair of adult breeders survives out of that clutch of two hundred eggs!

In exceptionally dry years, grasshoppers do famously, and more than ordinary numbers survive. After a couple of dry seasons, there may be great swarms of certain kinds that are capable of migrating in clouds for hundreds of miles and riddling the vegetation wherever they go. Wet years put a damper on the grasshopper economy, and their numbers may decline to far below average.

What, then, is the grasshopper's ecological position in its community? It is a creature that makes direct use of the great primary production of vegetation. Such animals are said to be operating a "key industry" which plays a critical role in supporting other kinds of animals. Common characteristics of key-industry species are these: they are small; they multiply rapidly; they use an abundant plant food supply; they are fed upon by other animals and therefore have a high loss rate. We can say that their job in this association of living things is to turn the tissues of plants into an animal food supply that can be used by other members of the community. In other words, the grasshopper is born to be the prey of its betters.

The female plains lubber grasshopper, a typical member of the shorthorn family, deposits a clutch of eggs in a shallow burrow in the ground. She may lay a dozen or more clutches, each containing upwards of a hundred eggs.

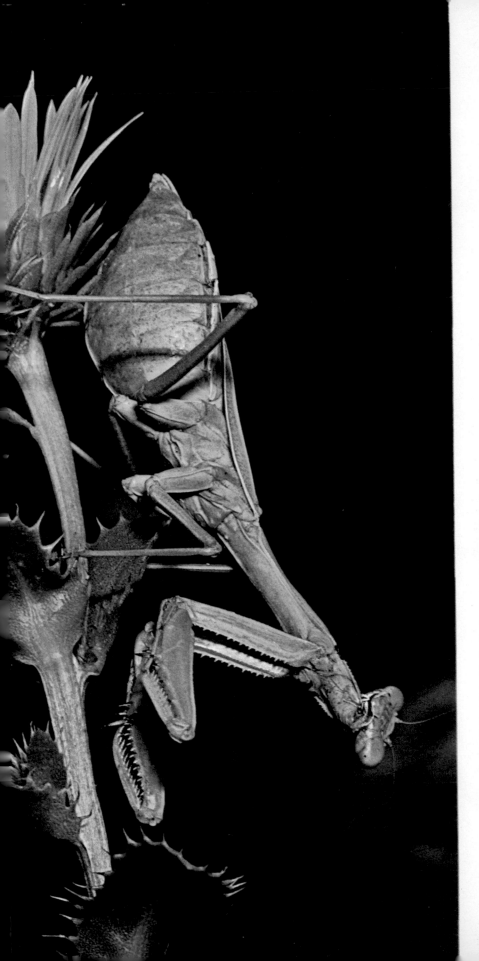

Not all insects are primary
consumers—many of
them are predators
that feed on primary
consumers. Perhaps the
most voracious of these
is the praying mantis
(*left*), which as a
quarter-inch nymph
attacks tiny plantlice and
as a five-inch adult
feasts on the largest
grasshoppers and crickets.
The robber fly (*right*)
seizes its prey in midair,
then carries it to a
convenient perch and
sucks its body juices.

Heavy industry

Insects of many kinds, including beetle larvae, or grubs, in the soil, caterpillars of various moths and butterflies, aphids, ants, true bugs, leafhoppers, and a world of others are working away at the plant food supply. To observe some of them we would do well to stretch out in the grass and see the situation from their level. We cannot watch for very long without realizing that the most important predators of this insect key industry are other insects.

These predatory insects are *secondary consumers.* They are less abundant than the plant eaters on which they feed. They occur in great variety—wasps, hornets, ants, ladybird beetles, dragonflies, robber flies, antlions, ground beetles, tiger beetles, and many more. Hard at work also are the eight-legged noninsects. Everywhere we see the nets that spiders have stretched for their victims. In hot southern ranges scorpions and tarantulas are highly capable predators. And, of course, there are many *vertebrate,* or backboned, animals that specialize in feeding on insects. Toads, lizards, and a wide variety of songbirds make use of this abundant food supply. With so many mouths to feed, the insect key industry must be a big operation in the community.

The little convergent ladybird beetle consumes enormous numbers of aphids and other small insects.

The relationship between the plants and insects of the grasslands is one of subtle give and take. At first glance, it might seem that insects do most of the taking: these aphids (*left*), for example, are sucking the sap from a coneflower stem. But the plants also benefit from the insects. On these sunflowers (*right*) the vital function of transferring pollen is being performed by flesh flies and a fritillary butterfly. Indeed, so interdependent are the flowering plants and the butterflies, moths, bees, and certain of the wasps and flies that their evolutionary history can be traced back side by side for 130 million years.

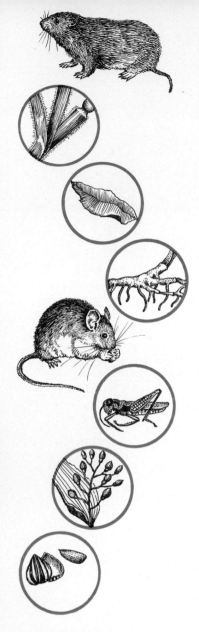

Another similar job is being carried out by the rodents. They feed directly on the vegetation and hence are primary consumers. We have seen that mice, in particular, tend to be of two types, leaf eaters and seed eaters. However, not all species fit such a neat classification. There are many mice, rats, and ground squirrels that have a more varied diet. They eat green shoots in season, and tubers and fleshy fruits when available. They store nuts and other seeds for winter, and they enjoy animal foods, such as insects, almost any time.

Nevertheless, certain species do typify certain habits, and the fat prairie vole is a good example. Being a leaf eater, it utilizes one of the most abundant food sources of the grasslands. It is extremely productive—a biologist will one day calculate that a single pair might, if the population suffered no losses at all, multiply to more than a million in a single year. Quite evidently, this meadow mouse performs efficiently the function of turning abundant plant foods into a high-protein ration for the predators.

In every habitat of the world we can see the key-industry creatures carrying out this critical "community service." In some environments, parallels with the grassland would be striking. For example, if we went north into the arctic tundra, we would find that the dense ground vegetation is not grasses, but primarily lichens. And there among the lichens is a short-tailed, stubby rodent consuming and multiplying at a great rate, to the benefit of foxes, hawks, owls, weasels, and other carnivores. This is the arctic lemming. It is doing the same kind of job in the same way as the prairie vole. These two animals occupy the same niche in their somewhat similar communities.

The prairie vole (*top*) is a leaf eater, feeding on grass stems, forb leaves, and tender roots and tubers. The prairie deer mouse (*bottom*), on the other hand, is typical of the seed eaters among the grassland mice: its preferred diet consists of grass seeds, fruit pits, sunflower seeds, and the like, plus insects such as grasshoppers. Both these creatures are active throughout the year, but each lays up an underground store of its favored foodstuffs to help tide it through the winter months when foraging is relatively poor.

The inside story of a buffalo

Because of their grazing and browsing habits, the bison and pronghorn must be classed as primary consumers. Of course, they are something special in being large of body and relatively slow multipliers. Also, they exemplify nicely a situation that is almost universal among these higher animals that use coarse vegetation (as against seeds and fruits) for food— they cannot digest it. To understand this, let us consider the "inside" story of a bison.

In reality, the digestive tract of a buffalo is a large fermentation vat populated by its own peculiar flora and fauna. The living things are mainly bacteria, but also one-celled animals of various kinds.

This microbial community does nearly the whole job of breaking down plant material eaten by the buffalo into soluble nutrients that can be absorbed, or forms that can be handled by the digestive juices of the animal.

Converting the dry brown forage of an October landscape into "more buffalo" is a lengthy process. The bison feed over relatively short periods and swallow grasses and other plants with little chewing. The food is stored in the rumen, a first stomach, where fermentation and softening up begin. Following feeding, during long periods of inactivity, the rumen contents are brought back up into the mouth, a "cud" at a time, and given a thorough chewing. The finely ground food then passes back through the rumen into three other chambers of the stomach. There chemical processing is largely completed before the usable nutrients go into the intestine for absorption.

In common with domestic cattle and other ruminants, the buffalo has a four-chambered stomach. In chambers 1 and 2, the rumen and reticulum, partially chewed plant material is stored and the process of digestion begins. The coarse plant parts are regurgitated and chewed as cud, then swallowed into chamber 3, the omasum, where excess water is removed. The resulting pulp then passes into chamber 4, the abomasum, where conventional digestion largely takes place.

In the stomachs of the bison there are bacteria to handle cellulose, fats, proteins—practically every component of a plant. These abundant one-celled organisms increase at a great rate, dividing every twenty to forty minutes. They produce a surplus of food solubles and vitamins and also contribute their own dead cells for digestion by the buffalo.

We called the buffalo a primary consumer. But the truth is there are consumers at an even more "primary" level within the buffalo itself. It is true of all the vegetation feeders that they must have this internal community to live. As we have seen, the jack rabbit produces two kinds of pellets, one only partly digested. It is thought that when a young jack rabbit eats the soft pellets of its mother, it gets a "starter" culture of the microbial life needed in its own intestine.

Living pyramid

Ecologists sometimes visualize the living things in a particular area as forming a pyramid. This could logically be a pyramid of numbers, a pyramid of mass (weight of living matter), or the total amount of the sun's energy that is tied up and transferred from one level of food consumption to another. The energy concept is most realistic. Biologists commonly think in these terms and speak of the steps in the pyramid as *trophic levels*.

It would be worth our while to look hard at the broad outlines of this pyramid and review a few points. First we have the physical setting of the ecosystem, on which soil, with all its own peculiar life forms, has developed. This is the base on which the steps of the community are stacked, one upon the other.

There are the primary producers, an assemblage of many different kinds of interacting and cooperating plants. Vegetation produces a large mass of new plant material each growing season.

A part of the great fund of vegetable nutrients is devoured by the primary consumers, commonly small herb-eating creatures. These first-level consumers are abundant and productive. They convert plant substance into animal form, which is acceptable food for the next trophic level.

The next level of the pyramid is composed of the secondary consumers, small predators that feed on the abundant plant eaters. They take only a part of the supply.

It would not be possible to say how many steps a pyramid of life should have. But at upper levels larger predators feed on the smaller ones and also on herbivores of larger size. In each upward step there is a great loss of energy,

The set of relationships through which food energy is passed upward to successively higher-order consumers can be likened to a pyramid. At the base of the grasslands pyramid of animal life is the immense mass of primary consumers, creatures which feed directly on plants and which range in size from tiny insects to the giant bison. At the peak of the pyramid is the relatively tiny mass of the highest-order predators—wolves, bears, and large predatory birds. Between peak and base are intermediate orders of consumers, each preying on one or more levels below and being preyed upon by one or more levels above. Many animals, because of their varied diet, must be shown on several levels: mice, for example, are both primary consumers of plants and secondary consumers of insects.

allowing only a small conversion to the higher trophic level. The mass of animal life declines rapidly in successive layers of the pyramid. On top of the theoretical heap is a species that is not commonly preyed upon by anything. This we can regard as the dominant carnivore of the community. In the grasslands it is usually the wolf.

Needless to say, all this is oversimplified. Not every creature fits such an idealized scheme. There are other local dominants such as the plains grizzly, the prairie falcon, and the golden eagle. The weasel belongs high in the pyramid as a capable meat eater, but it is small and sometimes falls prey to eagles and other predators. The bison does not fit the scheme either. It is a plant eater at the lowest level; yet it is the largest animal of North America and certainly few in number compared with key-industry creatures such as rodents and rabbits. Nature is never simple.

A band of bison enjoys the comforts of a dust wallow in the grassy foothills of the Rockies. Where the soil is thus disturbed, the hold of the grass on the soil is temporarily broken, allowing various invader plants to appear.

Plants with jobs

Earlier we saw how the bison helped to extend its habitat in forest edges by tearing up young trees. They "manage" their own habitat in other ways also. On the move, herds often march single file, cutting deep trails into the hillsides. In their frequent dust wallowing they dig their horns and hoofs into the soil, keeping it well stirred and bare. Then strong winds may help to create a "blow-out."

As we have recognized before, these "disturbance" sites have a critical relationship to the invader grasses and forbs, which we have seen in every part of the grassland. Many of these are *annuals*: they grow for a season, bear seed, and die. Typically they form a temporary healing growth over areas of bare ground and so seem to be Nature's means of protecting the soil in a hurry.

This photograph vividly illustrates what can happen when man tampers with the natural adjustments of plant life in the grassland. The boundary down the center of the picture is the survey line between two range properties near Taos, New Mexico. On the left, all the native sagebrush was grubbed out to "make room" for more grass. But the outcome was just the opposite, for the removal of the sagebrush allowed invasion by broomweed, which became dominant over most of the original grass. The end result is that the untouched range offers more grass than the "improved" range.

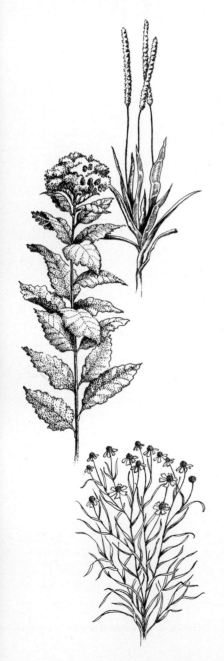

Here are three invader weeds that move in where the grass cover is disturbed: (*top to bottom*) woolly plantain, Baldwin ironweed, and bitter sneezeweed. None of these forbs offers acceptable forage for grazing animals, but all serve the useful function of holding the soil in place against erosion until more desirable species can reestablish themselves.

Following this initial stage, year by year the ground is taken over and stabilized against wind and water erosion by *perennial* grasses and other long-lived plants. These are characteristic of the more permanent and stable vegetation. Stable? Yes, in each region of the grasslands there is a complement of species that could maintain itself indefinitely if climatic conditions remained constant. This combination of plants is known as the *climax* vegetation.

But what happens during those extremes of weather, when it is exceptionally dry or wet? Several years of drought result in drastic changes in the relative abundance of different species. There are great losses among the climax grasses and an increase in so-called weeds. There is a shifting eastward of climax types that grow in drier country to the west. When conditions of higher rainfall return, there is a shift in the opposite direction; perennial grasses gain ground at the expense of the temporary kinds of cover. A plant ecologist of the twentieth century will find that a well-developed prairie in a series of near-average years will have only five percent annuals but ninety-five percent perennials.

Animal weeds

Now we must look closely to see something else. Wherever bare-ground conditions permit more broad-leaved herbs to grow, we get an increase of rabbits and hares, ground squirrels, and other rodents. With a few exceptions, such as the sod-inhabiting voles, these are creatures of the early stages of grassland vegetation. We can properly call them "animal weeds." These primary consumers are widespread, plentiful, and productive. Why do they not overrun their habitats and wipe out the food supplies?

As prey animals of the community, they tend to be kept within bounds. And there are other controlling factors, having to do with population density itself, which we shall examine. The changeability of weather is a factor that tends to produce ups and downs in year-to-year numbers.

But the truth is that there are times when these small animals do get out of hand. In periods of drought, as mentioned before, grasshoppers may darken the sun in great moving hordes that strip bare the vegetation in their path. Or after a couple of seasons of heavy moisture, mice may run wild in a particular region, with hundreds per acre blighting the grass. When this happens, predators may concentrate and reduce the population.

Jack rabbits of the southern plains are particularly likely to increase vastly in a few favorable years. The overflowing numbers thin out their food supply, pollute their environment, promote the spread of disease, attract a concentration of predators, and set the stage in every detail for a sharp decline. In the wild, overprosperity is not prosperity at all. The community does not tolerate great abundance for long.

Flesh feeders

We noted that carnivores are at work at higher levels in the living pyramid. As compared with the prey animals, predators are commonly large in size, or they make up for a relatively small size in speed, agility, and other qualities appropriate to their profession. They are smaller in number than their prey. We could not possibly have as many foxes as rabbits, could we? Since their losses are lower, the hunters do not need to multiply so rapidly; and indeed they do not.

Nature designed the fed-upon creatures to convert the tissues of plants into animal form for the support of the meat eaters. But she gave the predators a corresponding function—to thin out the plant feeders and thus prevent the basic foods of the community from being destroyed. If this seems to be going in circles, perhaps it is. One thing depends upon the other, and these associated animals and plants are in a closed system of controls.

There is another way in which the food relationships in a wild community can be visualized. Each trophic level can be regarded as a link in a chain. So a certain *food chain* might be expressed this way: plant—grasshopper—meadowlark—falcon. Another might be seeds—prairie deer mouse—weasel—coyote; or again, grass—vole—striped skunk—golden eagle.

Each of these food chains illustrates that the pyramid of life includes several levels of meat-eating consumers. Certainly at a low level are those predacious insects we spoke of, especially the abundant ants, beetles, and the like, many of which are eaten by birds and other larger animals.

Each plant and animal of the grassland community is a "link" in one or more food chains such as the simple one shown here: plant life provides sustenance for the vole, which is eaten by the skunk, which in turn is preyed upon by the golden eagle.

147

In this typical prairie food chain, plant seeds are consumed by the prairie deer mouse, which is preyed upon by the weasel, which in turn becomes prey of the coyote.

Probably it is not a regular occurrence that the weasel is taken by a coyote or that a striped skunk becomes the prey of an eagle. But the larger carnivores do occasionally take the smaller ones, and this represents the dominance of one link in the chain over another.

The dominant meat eaters are the few in every range that have almost nothing to fear from natural enemies; the wolf is one example. In the badlands, the white bear has a similar position of security. Where both of them occur, they simply avoid trouble. These animals are at the far-right end of their food chains, and they occupy that little block on top of the pyramid of life.

Enemies within

Are there animals without enemies? It seems unlikely in the life community, where there are checks and balances to keep everything within certain limits.

The carnivores, big and powerful though some of them are, do have a threat hanging over them, awaiting the right conditions to strike. This threat is posed by the parasites and other disease organisms that are carried by every creature, most of which seem to be satisfactorily healthy.

Under ordinary conditions they are healthy. But let them suffer a food scarcity and malnutrition; or expose them to a long period of bad weather; or permit them to become too abundant for a while, which leads to social unrest, competition, and fighting. Then the individual loses its resistance to disease, and some fatal contagion is likely to spread. Meat-eating mammals are prone to diseases of the nervous system that men of the future will call by such names as encephalitis, rabies, and distemper. An overabundance of nearly any species may lead to an unusual spread of mange.

Like the animals they feed upon, the carnivores are subject to regular annual losses and the replacement of population. And all individual predators are not equal in capability. As in every species, including man, some are stupid or lazy, and something is likely to happen to these. Actually starvation is not uncommon among the wild hunters. They are likely to thrive when prey is abundant and decline when it is scarce. In truth, the plant feeders control their predators to a much greater degree than the predators control the plant feeders.

Among insects we see some of the most striking parasitic forms, which have tied their life cycles to particular host species that they exploit for their own survival. For example, we would do well to follow a medium-sized bumble bee darting over the prairie swards. It disappears into the grasses and, as we watch closely, into the side of the grass nest of a prairie vole. This nest was built last winter under the snow and is abandoned. Well, not exactly abandoned, because now it houses a thriving colony of bumble bees, complete with honey pots, pollen cells, and cocoons from which workers are emerging. A queen bumble bee hibernated through last winter and founded this colony in the spring. Now she is laying eggs to build up her family.

The bee we followed is a fertile queen, but not *the* queen. She is a parasitic bumble bee that moved into the colony, lived quietly for a few days, and then displaced or possibly killed the original queen. She laid her own eggs in the nursery cells, and workers fed the new and alien generation at the expense of their own kind. The parasitic bumble bee has no workers of its own species and is totally dependent on this reproductive piracy.

Practically every abundant and influential species among the grassland insects is supporting a thriving assortment of well-adjusted parasitic freeloaders which help to hold its numbers in check. The adaptations of parasites commonly are highly complicated, indicating many millions of years in the making of the association.

The June bugs, or May beetles, that swarm into the fires of Indian camps on warm spring evenings are carrying a typical burden. Among the flights there are pyrgota flies moving with unerring swiftness. One of them will poise over the back of a flying female beetle whose protective outer wings are spread, exposing the soft surface of her upper abdomen. The fly darts down, and its needlelike ovipositor pierces the beetle, leaving an egg beneath the skin. Knocked to the ground, the beetle takes wing again and sails away to feed. She spends her days buried in the ground.

In about five days the fly egg has hatched, and the larva is living from the tissues and fluids of the beetle. Life for the plagued host slows down, and finally there is an eve-

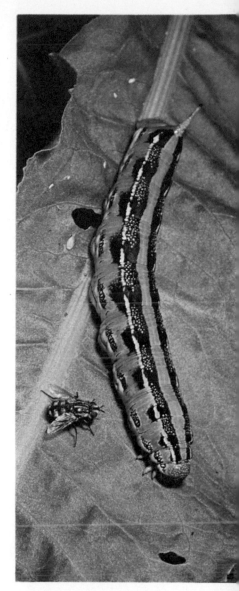

The hornworm caterpillar, here feeding on a dock leaf, and the tachina fly, a not-too-distant relative of the house fly, are the principals in a relationship somewhat more complicated than that of the eater and the eaten.

DEADLY PASSENGERS

The tachina fly, over the course of countless generations, has evolved a unique system for assuring the perpetuation of its kind. The female tachina attaches its eggs to a living host; upon hatching, the larval flies burrow into the flesh of the host and proceed to eat it literally from the inside out. Caterpillars are by no means the tachina's only victims: there are many species of the fly, and each has its preferred host, chosen from among insects, spiders, centipedes, and woodlice. But caterpillars are the most common of the host animals, not only for the tachina flies but for certain species of wasps that also parasitize them. However, some caterpillars have evolved poisonous or sticky bristles, which ward off the attacks of these deadly pests.

Having located her victim and selected a site upon its body, the female tachina fly (above left) swings her ovipositor into position and begins carefully affixing her eggs, one at a time, to the hapless hornworm (above right).

fi
b
A
dr

a
ing
Th
hap
floc
stru
bor

I
floc
part
divi
the

If
vari
man
life
whic
tion
right
the a

Fourteen eggs now adorn the hornworm; as they hatch, the larval flies will burrow into the caterpillar's body and slowly consume it. The hornworm will die slowly, living long enough to give the tachina fly's offspring a good start in life.

Two
with
rabb
by c
slow
inbo
culli
helps
speci

physically or mentally—diseased, injured, or otherwise handicapped.

The more we see of predation in this system of Nature, the more it is evident that something orderly and useful is going on between the primary consumers and their enemies. Probably it is tied in closely with seasonal changes in the numbers of animals.

The season of production, of course, is spring and summer, when prey species are breeding and storing up a surplus of their own number which must last through the unproductive fall and winter. A breeding stock of adequate size must be left for another year. It is clear enough that the warm season brings a renewal of the plant-food supply, and hence the habitat has its highest capacity to support the great increase of animal life.

This habitat capacity does not remain great: by early winter both food and cover have been reduced, a process that continues through to the end of the cold season. One might say that from midsummer to April, on any hundred acres of prairie or plain, there must be a decline in the number of animals of a given kind that can live in comfort and safety. As the year progresses and conditions change, each jack rabbit or antelope must seek out the best foods in the safest situations in order to survive. And in those favored spots it finds other jack rabbits or antelope doing the same.

Now comes the eagle, which finds that there are too many jack rabbits for the remaining "best" situations. Some of the jacks are not well accommodated; they must move about frequently in poor cover, much to the advantage of the eagle. The meat-eating bird helps reduce the population, most particularly the jack rabbits that are least able to compete and are taking the leavings in the habitat.

That means, of course, that by spring only the most durable and capable jack rabbits are left. By means of the predator, Nature has selected her breeding stock to pass on its superior survival characteristics to the next generation. This is a merciless system for the weak and unwary. But it develops a strong race, and this is the key to success over the

A jack rabbit becomes a meal for a golden eagle and its young. Our populations of predatory birds have been greatly reduced by often well-meaning but misguided humans. The loss of these big birds invariably upsets Nature's system of checks and balances, and all wildlife suffers.

155

A kangaroo rat, a primary consumer, has converted the primary production of green plants into animal substances. Those substances are now passed on to a group of second-order consumers, a brood of young burrowing owls.

dise
To
the

T
They
resp
Pred
food
their

Or
game
can s
bers
fail,
must

Ou
anima
Abov
be ta
level
illustr
perity

But
scale
Thus
anima
use a
the en

A PRAIRIE FOOD CHAIN

Pictured on these two pages are three links in a prairie food chain: kangaroo rat, burrowing owl, and gopher snake. The events shown in these photographs are perhaps not attractive by human standards, but judgments of "cruelty" and "right" do not apply here. These are simply animals living—and dying—as Nature has equipped them to do, and in so doing they are automatically adjusting their populations to sizes compatible with the environment they inhabit. Predation is a necessary and important aspect of a balanced wildlife community, and where man has eliminated it, the preyed-upon species have suffered— often from starvation and disease following an explosive population increase.

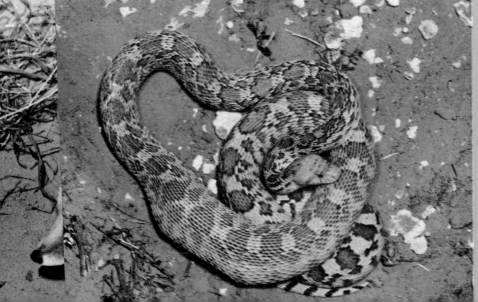

The chain continues in the series of three photographs to the left as one of the young burrowing owls is swallowed by a third-order consumer, a gopher snake. The chain may not end here: we can easily imagine the snake falling victim to a fourth-order consumer, a peccary, perhaps; and the peccary becoming the prey of a fifth-order consumer—a human with a rifle.

Returns to the soil

In a manner of speaking, we have been taking the grassland
community apart to see how it operates. It seems to be a
well-organized system that captures energy from the sun
by combining the hydrogen of water with carbon dioxide,
and subsequently nitrogen from the air, in the living substance of plants and animals. A vast array of highly complex organic compounds is passed through the food linkages
of the community to a final stage represented by a few
carnivores.

We have emphasized that, at each step in the transfer of
energy from one level of consumption to the next, relatively
little of the available mass is used. The grasshopper, meadow mouse, and bison, on the average, take only a small
part of the total available vegetation. Many plants are not
grazed heavily, and the bulk of them will die and be returned to the soil. Whether their tissues are used to feed an
herbivore or whether they simply rot, the process is one of

A pair of coyotes feast on the
remains of an elk that could not
make it through the rigors of
the winter. In the wild it is the
destiny of most animals to be
eaten. The activity of coyotes,
vultures, and other scavengers
and decomposers is vital to
the general welfare of the
natural community.

oxidation—combining oxygen from the air with the great variety of carbon compounds that make up living things. The carbon and oxygen go back into the air as carbon dioxide, which is again available for the growth of plants. Other products of decomposition are the soluble salts that find their way into soil water and become nutrients for the next generation of plants. Through photosynthesis, oxygen is again set free by the plants and is used by animals. It will also be used by bacteria that accomplish a large part of the breakdown of plant and animal bodies.

Here we are dealing with another big class of organisms, the *decomposers*. Sooner or later, every part of every living thing will be destroyed, disassembled, and reduced to its chemical building blocks. We can see the beginning of this process as we watch an old bull buffalo standing unsteadily by himself on the plain, surrounded by a dozen wolves. What happens to him will be a clue to how many of the decomposers work. The bull is an ancient sire that could no longer abide the social pressure of the young bulls in the

summer breeding herd. So he became a loner, living by himself and enjoying the bare ground of a prairie-dog colony, where he could wallow in the comfort of abundant dust. He grew stiff with age, gaunt on a diet of inferior forage, and nearly blind. The wolves cannily sensed his condition and gathered around to appraise him more carefully. What they found was encouraging—this was the old bull's time. They injured a hind leg and now keep him standing and unable to feed or water. As he weakens, they will finish the job.

Let us look at the scene a few days later, after the wolves have fed and gone off to lie around on a grassy knoll. Following their departure a troop of scavenging coyotes close in to eat the tough parts and help scatter the bones. Buz-

George Catlin, an American painter who traveled up the Missouri River in the mid-nineteenth century, perhaps overdramatized the death struggle between a wolf pack and a bison. The wolves would more likely spend several days worrying the old bull until he was weakened enough for a safe and easy kill.

zards drop out of the sky to have their turn; as they poke their heads and necks into the bloody body cavity, we can see why it is an advantage for vultures to have bare heads. After all, head feathers cannot be groomed with the bill.

The site of the kill is a great spot of hair and wool, in the midst of which is partly chewed plant material from the old bull's stomachs. Gnawed bones are being cleaned up and dragged around. The ribs are nearly all eaten. Here are the articulated legs, the jaw, and part of the skull with the rows of upper teeth.

As we move the partly cleaned spine of the bison, we see that moist areas under patches of hide are crawling with white fly larvae, or maggots, and carrion beetles arc every-where at work. A large piece of the thick neck skin has been

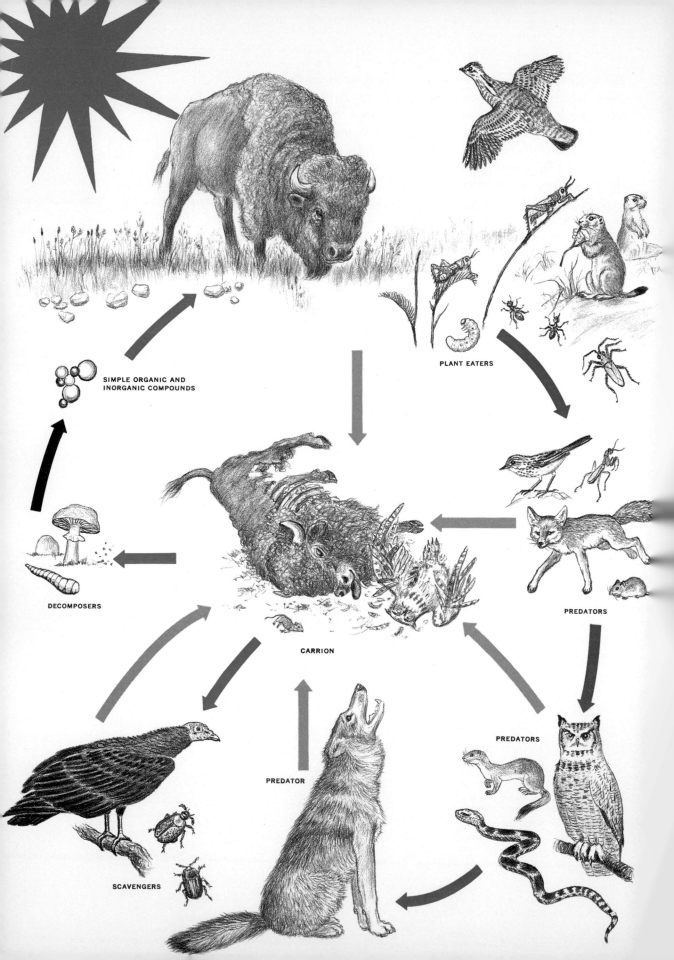

SIMPLE ORGANIC AND
INORGANIC COMPOUNDS

PLANT EATERS

DECOMPOSERS

CARRION

PREDATORS

PREDATORS

PREDATOR

SCAVENGERS

hauled off to one side, and as we move it a swarm of black crickets is exposed. Though they are usually plant feeders, the crickets have an obvious liking for the hair and hide.

All the animals that feed on the old bull's remains are using digestible parts to furnish the proteins and fats that build their bodies. They also oxidize the products of digestion to release energy on which their bodies operate, thus converting the trapped sun power to their own use. Carbon dioxide is given off to the air. Undigested materials, principally bone and hair, are deposited on the ground as droppings. Insects and bacteria work on these, reducing them to forms that, with the next rain, go into the humus of the soil.

The more resistant bones last longer, but in the course of months or years these will be chiseled away by the rodents, especially calcium-hungry pregnant females. Bone phosphate will be tied up in the abundant organic matter of the grassland soil and then will become available for use in that first step of the basic plant-growth process, photosynthesis.

It is easy to see the many kinds of decomposers at work on the old bull. What we do not see is even more important, for the soil under the grassland is a vast and complex community of decomposers. Insects of many kinds, especially ants, ground beetles, dung beetles, and carrion beetles, are there, as are sowbugs, millipedes, nematodes, mites, earthworms, and many others—feeding, digesting, excreting, dying. Plants are fundamentally involved in the breakdown and "mineralizing" of organic matter. The black humus is a network of filaments of simple fungi, and it is loaded with bacteria, yeasts, and algae of kinds unknown and unnumbered. Of this we may be sure: each has its place and does its useful job in the cycling of nutrients through which life is sustained in this grassland ecosystem.

The plants and animals of the grasslands are interlinked in a complex system by means of which the basic chemicals of life are constantly recycled. Using the energy of the sun, the plants convert simple substances into foodstuffs. These are first eaten by the primary consumers and then, through predation, passed on to successively higher-order consumers (*yellow arrows*). Eventually all animals, large and small, become carrion (*green arrows*). The decomposers then complete the cycle by reducing the dead tissue once again to simple organic and inorganic compounds (*black arrow*).

Our overview

We have seen no creature that is not a part of one of the many types of grassland communities. Each has a way of living that depends on its associated plants and animals. Certainly all communities are responding to the gradual changes that take place over long periods of time, especially changes in climate. They must respond also to alterations in site and soil brought about by the living things themselves. Thus, the prairie gradually built up a store of fertility unequaled by any other environment.

As we reflect on the significance of this intricate organization, it dawns on us that no living thing can be preserved for any length of time outside its own natural community. The reason is that when major conditions of the environment are altered, the old process of natural selection takes a new direction. In the course of time, we shall no longer have the same plant or animal that grew in the original association.

To carry this reasoning further, it is evident that our learning and our science will benefit from keeping sample primitive areas in which plant and animal life is left to work out its existence in the ancient manner. If we do this, we shall always have the means of learning from Nature. We shall likewise have the original species that might at any time be needed for special and practical purposes.

We have learned many things from looking carefully at this grassland of 1491. However, even in the mid-twentieth century, it would be foolish to suppose that men will have more than just begun to understand the complicated communities of the prairies and plains. And certainly there can never be an end to the search for such knowledge.

A bleaching bison skull serves as a reminder that the fate of all living creatures of the grasslands, as elsewhere, is ultimately the return to the soil. Nothing is ever really consumed in Nature—it is only borrowed for a while.

Men of

Yesterday

We could not travel far on these grasslands of the fifteenth century without seeing man and his works. Some tens of thousands of years ago, ancestors of the Indian must have arrived, like the bison, as immigrants from Asia. It is almost certain that both crossed the Bering Strait land bridge and moved southward through the unglaciated interior of Alaska. Now the various peoples are scattered to the southern tip of South America.

In the region of prairies and plains we find them principally on watercourses and timbered borderlands. In this period it is clear that man is largely an "edge" creature. He needs in his habitat the variety furnished by different vegetation types. Wherever they live, the men of this early day are gatherers of the edible roots, berries, fruits, and nuts that grow in their home area. Likewise they are all hunters. They stalk elk and deer in brush and timberlands, and they take smaller creatures when necessary. For this hunting to be successful, the game must be plentiful and not frequently disturbed. Snares, deadfalls, and the bow and arrow kill animals one at a time; they are not "mass producers" of food.

The greatest food resource to be found anywhere is on the open plain, where there are millions of bison for the taking. Probably none of these ancient Indians has ever made full use of this rich resource. Yet they are working at it. Let us look more closely to see how human problems are being solved in and around this vast grassland habitat.

The old villagers

Frequently, in our journeys along the Missouri River, we have seen palisaded villages of large earthen lodges. The inhabitants probably are the most advanced people in the entire region of the grass, since they are favorably situated and have a successful agriculture. They raise limited crops of corn, beans, squash, sunflowers, and tobacco. Tribes that will be known in a later era as Mandan, Arikara, Hidatsa, and Kansa spend the bitter winters in their substantial lodges. They have pottery for cooking and storage, large pits for caching surplus food, and other items associated with settled agricultural folk.

These villagers have not forgotten the old ways, and for their pursuit of the buffalo they have developed a specialized double life. It begins in spring, when the squaws plant their gardens in areas of rich soil scattered over the river bottom. With seed in the ground, they abandon their crops to the elements and head westward onto the grassland for a long summer hunt. On a late spring morning we may see them heading out.

The village bustles with activity as piles of packs and bundles are assembled outside the lodges. Each of the many dogs must bear a burden lashed to its back or tied between two dragging poles; later French trappers will call this conveyance a *travois*. Anything left over must be carried by the squaws, and so the rule of the day is to travel light. In small groups the Indians scatter out onto the prairie.

Now the river people are back to a hunting and food-gathering culture. They have left their comfortable lodges behind and must use their summer shelters, small cone-shaped tepees of hides stretched over the travois poles. For killing antelope they are dependent largely on the bow and arrow, and they hunt by careful stalking. They take buffalo in the same manner, but where the terrain is favorable they also stage mass drives to impound entire bands of buffalo in dead-end arroyos or man-made pens. A herd may be stampeded over a sheer drop where many animals will be killed or injured. Commonly the bison bands are on the move, cropping the grass where it is good and then shifting to new pastures. The men must follow, but with difficulty, for their dog transportation is slow.

Nonetheless, the villagers manage to penetrate far across the plains. Archeologists of the future will find their tools and artifacts clear to the mountains. The various tribes wander largely within their own hunting territories, and as autumn approaches they are turning eastward again. If summer rains have favored them, there will be crops to harvest and store for the winter ahead. They have fresh supplies of skins and as much dried meat as can be carried.

In a George Catlin painting, two Indians use wolf-hide disguises to work within bow-and-arrow range of a buffalo herd. This type of hunting required an intimate understanding of the big animal's habits and temperament.

Hunts of autumn

In the course of our travels, we have had evidence of men living permanently on the western side of the great grassland. At nearly any time of year, bands of hunters may be encountered pursuing the buffalo. Throughout the central and southern plains, crops are growing on favorable sites in the stream bottoms. We can guess that in dry years the harvests are poor in this sun-baked highland.

Let us follow northward along the mountains into the northwest plains—country that will be central Montana. In this region of short growing seasons the signs of Indian agriculture diminish greatly. The people living here depend heavily on gathering and hunting. We cannot be sure who they are, for in centuries to come there will be a great shifting around as various tribes move westward. That they have a choice hunting ground is evident. The area provides elk, deer, and mountain sheep, in addition to an abundance of bison. And for the mass slaughter of buffalo it is well equipped with fine natural sites that have been used for thousands of years. Anthropologists will call these *buffalo jumps.*

The operation of a buffalo jump requires cooperation by an entire village. No doubt this method is used whenever the opportunity arises, but it is most valuable in the fall, when cows and calves are fat and their robes thickened with wool. This is something we must see.

It is an evening in October, and as we follow along a river flood plain an abrupt escarpment rises on our left. Above, the grassland stretches northward to distant hills. Fires twinkle among trees in the shadow of the cliffs. This is a temporary camp of skin tepees and lean-tos.

Before one of these shelters a squaw is heating small stones in a fire. A green animal skin lines a bucket-sized pit in the ground, and in this crude kettle a thick soup is bubbling. Using sticks as tongs, the woman places hot rocks in the stew and deftly removes them for reheating in the fire.

These Indians are "stone boilers." They have only crude pottery and little basketry. They use the bow and arrow, the lance, and other stone, bone, and wood implements. They chip projectile heads from chert, obsidian, and other materials. They kindle their fires with a drill spun between the hands.

A camp such as this must be moved frequently to new hunting and gathering grounds, but there is no way to carry anything really heavy. As elsewhere, the limitations of dog

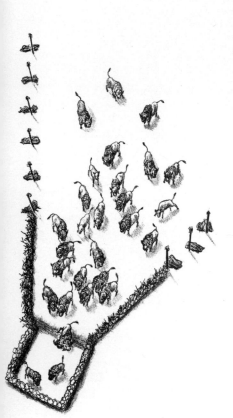

Here is another buffalo-hunting technique employed by the Indians before the advent of the horse. A three-sided stone corral was first built; the fourth side consisted of an earthen ramp flanked by two converging walls of brush. These walls were extended by rows of Indians crouching beneath buffalo skins and holding fifteen-foot poles topped with buffalo dung. It was then a relatively easy matter to drive the buffalo into the corral, where, powerless to escape, they could be killed and butchered at leisure.

transportation largely determine how the people can live.

The group we are watching came to this campsite quietly in the afternoon to take advantage of a great opportunity. Young men scouting the highland came in on the run to report that several hundred buffalo are grazing toward the east. As would be expected, it is a mixed herd; the older bulls have not yet separated into their bachelor groups for wintering. The animals are moving toward a side canyon that comes down from the north to join the main river valley where the camp is located. If the buffalo continue in this direction, they will be funneled between two hills toward a steep drop-off of the canyon wall.

Long before daylight, all able-bodied Indians leave the camp and move to appointed stations on the plain above. Soon after sunrise we can see what is happening. The bison have been grazing, but now they become restless and drift eastward more rapidly. Occasionally an Indian shows himself behind them on a rise, just enough to keep the herd moving without real alarm. Ahead, the strategy unfolds.

The herd could easily turn northward and flee across the open plain. But every few hundred feet along that side of their route are low piles of rocks that form a long line stretching toward the drop-off ahead. This is one side of a great V, for on the south a shorter line follows the foot of a low hillside. The two lines converge at the brink of the cliff, where they are only fifty yards apart. On each side are larger rock piles and even brush and trees hauled from the stream margin below and arranged to form a flimsy fence.

The light is improving, and now we can see something else. Behind each of the rock piles an Indian is lying on the ground, covered by a skin. The stones give small concealment, but in the dark they probably served to mark the proper hiding place of each person in the barrier lines, between which the buffalo now are beginning to move at a fast walk.

The pace increases as more Indians emerge on the plain behind the buffalo. The leaders of the herd, several old cows trailing their blocky calves, hesitate and veer to the left. But behind the markers figures quickly rise, waving their robes, and the animals head back to the east. Suddenly they break into a full stampede.

Squaws and young men are standing on each side now, urging the buffalo into the narrowing path ahead. Their yells can be heard amid the pounding of hoofs. A great roll

In a 1947 painting, William R. Leigh recreates a buffalo jump, with scores of the big grazers stampeded to destruction by a tribe of plains Indians. The artist has depicted several stages of the operation which in fact would not have been carried on simultaneously. Probably the whole tribe would have first joined in the job of starting and directing the stampede. The tasks of butchering, dressing, and drying the carcasses in the valley below would have been undertaken later at leisure—and without the risk of being crushed by a two-thousand-pound buffalo. The Indians used this method of buffalo hunting thousands of years before horses were introduced into their culture. And even in the seventeenth century and later, after their introduction into the plains, horses probably played little part in the drives at buffalo jumps.

of dust goes up to obscure the fleeing herd, but we are directly overhead as they reach the cliffside in a headlong rush. The animals in front lurch wildly to right and left to avoid the fall. But they are bowled over and trampled in the irresistible crush of the charging herd. The dark mass plunges over the edge in a mighty Niagara of hurtling bodies. They strike the rocks forty feet below and tumble down the talus slope to the grassy flat.

A short time later the Indians move their camp to a spot near the butchering. For many days the skinning and dressing of hides goes on. Racks of drying meat smoke above the fires, and leg bones are splintered and boiled for marrow fat. Everyone in the band, including the wolfish dogs, feeds many times a day while abundance lasts. It is likely these people will head toward a winter camp built of logs and earth in some sheltered valley. This means that some heavy hauling must be done. The buffalo jump should be left undisturbed for future use. As another reality, the odor is becoming unbearable.

Man in the food chain

If we were to excavate the deep layer of bones, hair, and horns that has collected at the foot of this jump, it would be evident that thousands of bison have been driven to destruction here. Along the north-south ranges of the Rocky Mountains, this is the principal way of killing large numbers of buffalo. However, the method is widely varied and adapted to local situations. Commonly a herd may be driven over a low barrier or drop-off into a slaughtering "pound" fenced with rocks or other barriers. There are many such killing grounds on the more level prairies eastward. In winter the animals can occasionally be overtaken and killed in deep snow. When ice goes out of northern rivers, there is much work to be done, for thousands of drowned buffalo are floating downstream. Then the Indian becomes a scavenger and enjoys the abundance while he may.

Shattered buffalo bones trace the course of a dry gulch used by ancient plains Indians as a buffalo jump some 8500 years ago. Careful excavation of this remarkable archeological site, 140 miles southeast of Denver, Colorado, revealed much about the Indians' hunting and butchering methods.

This badly distorted skeleton of a young buffalo was one of thirty-nine animals that were buried in the bottom of the dry gulch by the bodies of buffalo that followed them. They remained intact, because the Indians were unable to get to them for butchering. The presence of days-old calves in the buffalo jump indicates that the hunt took place in spring.

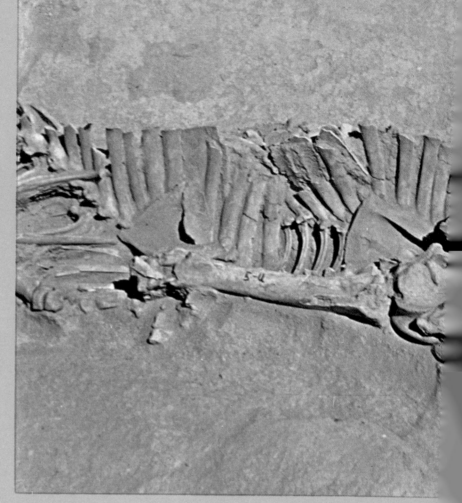

Projectile points such as this one, still lodged against the backbone that stopped it eight thousand years ago, were attached to long wooden shafts and hurled at the buffalo, sometimes from a throwing stick.

A PREHISTORIC BUFFALO HUNT

In late 1957, two amateur archeologists, Sigurd Olsen and Gerald Chubbuck, stumbled upon a meandering path of buffalo bones sticking out of the shortgrass plains soil in eastern Colorado. They had discovered all the evidence necessary to piece together the fascinating story of a plains Indian hunt that took place more than eighty centuries ago. An archeological team from the University of Colorado Museum estimates that in about 6500 B.C. a band of some 150 Indians staged a spectacular stampede of the now extinct buffalo *Bison occidentalis* over the brink of a dry gulch. The total take: 46 adult bulls, 63 adult cows, 27 young bulls, 38 young cows, and 16 calves. The Indians hauled most of the carcasses to open ground and expertly butchered them, tossing the stripped bones back into the gully. Over a period of years the trench filled up with earth. There the bones lay buried until erosion exposed them thousands of years later.

Excavation yielded forty-seven artifacts of the ancient hunters, including twenty-seven skillfully flaked flint projectile points.

These dramatic scenes of the fifteenth century suggest that the human culture can go in two directions. On the one hand is the settled existence of the agriculturalist. Domesticated plants make it possible to raise large quantities of food, and people feed at a low level in the pyramid of life. They are primary consumers, and large populations can be supported on favorable lands. The alternative habit is that of the hunter, which places man at the top of the pyramid in the position of a dominant carnivore.

Actually, like the great white bear, the early grassland people have a combination diet. Within climatic limits, farming efforts of the squaws produce remarkably well. Wild herbs and fruits are nearly always available somewhere. Where terrain and the movements of bison favor, the methods of mass killing are amazingly ingenious and productive. Yet we cannot doubt that there are periods of want and privation, especially when the parching winds of drought blister the open lands for several years running.

On the plains, as we have seen, there is a great bounty of buffalo. Certainly these tens of millions could support many more people if they were readily available. But the Indian's use of the bison is limited by his transportation, for he can-

The modern horse traces its ancestry back to *Hyracotherium,* a terrier-sized creature of the North American forests of sixty million years ago. This "dawn horse" had four-toed forefeet and teeth adapted to browsing on soft plant parts. In time, the descendants of *Hyracotherium* left the forest and took to life on the plains, a change that necessitated sturdier teeth for grazing and faster feet for fleeing from predators. *Orohippus* shows the beginning of these changes; *Mesohippus* displays significantly heavier teeth and three-toed feet. . . .

not follow the herds at will and carry with him the paraphernalia of an abundant life. More particularly, he cannot live like the wolf, making use of the steady production of overage and vulnerable animals. Man's large-scale killing is indiscriminate, taking animals of both sexes and all ages alike, and it may well be that this is his most important "unnatural" influence on this wild community.

There are others to follow. In fact, something is to happen that will greatly alter the relationships of the Indian on the plains. We must follow along to witness these events.

Return of the horse

Some sixty million years ago, at the end of the age of dinosaurs, the Rocky Mountains reared skyward, blocking the flow of moist air from the Pacific Ocean. The mid-portion of the continent became increasingly dry. The age of mammals was on. There was a great and spectacular succession of plant-eating beasts in the region of North America that was to become our prairies and plains.

Among the earliest of these creatures was the first known

... *Merychippus*, also three-toed, definitely displays true grazing teeth. In *Pliohippus* the one-toed hoof has clearly emerged, with only vestiges of the extra two toes. Finally, in the last million years, the modern horse *Equus* appeared, but for uncertain reasons—possibly epidemic disease—vanished from the continent about 25,000 years ago. By that time, however, it had spread to Asia and thence to Europe, and was reintroduced to the land of its genesis by the Spanish explorers less than four centuries ago.

Merychippus

Pliohippus

Equus

The introduction of the horse to the grasslands in the early seventeenth century revolutionized the Indian's way of life. This George Catlin sketch shows Pawnees capturing and breaking wild horses, which spread rapidly over the grasslands after the coming of the Spaniards.

ancestor of the horse—*Hyracotherium*, a five-toed browsing animal the size of a small dog. This creature gave rise to all the horse types, many of which became extinct, while others formed the parent line of modern horses.

As millions of years wore on, the horse ancestors increased in size. The outside toes weakened and disappeared, and the nail on the middle toe became a hoof. The teeth became increasingly adapted to grinding rather than crushing. The first grazing horse was the three-toed *Merychippus*, which lived twenty-odd million years ago. By the relatively recent time of the last glaciation, North America was the home of a true horse. And at a time when glacial ice lay thick over the northeastern part of the continent—when sea level was much lower than now, because much of the earth's water was in icecaps—the horse was spreading westward over the Bering Strait land bridge to Asia. There it might well have encountered bison or men headed toward their mission in the New World.

No one knows why, but some thousands of years ago the horse disappeared from this continent. It was not seen here again until Spanish conquerors brought their steeds of war to Mexico in the early 1500s. These were horses of excellent stock, part Arab and adapted to living in semiarid grasslands.

By the early 1600s, breeding stocks of horses had reached

the frontier, and Santa Fe became a center of trade with neighboring Indians. The red men soon learned to ride. In the century to follow, the use of the horse spread northward, eventually to all the people of the grasslands. Some of the horses went wild, living and increasing as did their ancestors on these same horizons of grass.

Among the first tribes to adopt the horse were the Apaches, who also used them extensively as food. About 1700, a tribal offshoot of the Shoshones moved southward behind the Rockies and emerged onto the plains of New Mexico. These, the Comanches, mastered the horse culture and forced the Apaches into brush country to the west. On eastern borders of the grassland and far north into Canada, a general westward movement of woodland peoples was under way as the pressure from white settlements grew. The plains were invaded by tribes whose wealth and power built up rapidly. Cheyenne, Arapaho, Sioux, Crow, and Blackfoot

The acquisition of the horse provided the Indian with the one thing that he had lacked to exploit the full potential of the grasslands: complete mobility. Freed from the slowness and limited capacity of the dog travois (*top*), he could now carry the gear of an enriched culture by horse travois (*bottom*) and more easily follow the great buffalo herds across the open plains.

In another 1832 painting, Catlin showed this Sioux hunting party in hot pursuit of a bison herd. Note the rawhide line trailing behind each horse. The painter explained its purpose: "In running the buffaloes . . . the *laso* drags on the ground at the horse's feet, and sometimes several rods behind, so that if a man is dismounted, which is often the case, by the tripping or the stumbling of the horse, he has the power of grasping to the laso, and by stubbornly holding onto it, of stopping and securing his horse, on whose back he is instantly replaced, and continuing on the chase."

band of rawhide or horsehair encircles the chest. Under this the rider slips a knee on each side, effectively anchoring himself to his excited and prancing mount. Each hunter carries a bow and quiver of arrows or a long lance.

Quietly the party rides up the steep bank and onto the level prairie. Instantly they break into a charge, for the buffalo are now only two hundred yards away. The herd wheels and dashes away in a mad rush as the fresh horses close the distance from behind.

The hunters press by a few lumbering bulls and on into the dust cloud that screens the fleeing animals. A brave on a fine-limbed pinto leans to the left, steering his responsive steed to the side of a nimble wild-eyed cow. At the critical instant he thrusts his lance into the ribcage of the cow and

withdraws it as his horse leaps away. The cow drops back, and herd and hunters pound on in a riot of action and excitement.

Here another rider leans over his horse's neck with bowstring drawn to his cheek. The arrow streaks downward and sinks to the feathers into the side of a sleek heifer. Quickly another arrow is out of the quiver and strung as the hunter looks for his next victim. Only well-conditioned females are taken, for these furnish the fat meat and lightweight hides that mean good living for the human predator.

After a chase of nearly a mile, the horsemen turn their blown mounts back along the route. Twenty-odd buffalo are scattered over the plain. Some are down and await

At the left, two mounted Indians attack a tending pair with a calf; below a single brave prepares to send an arrow into a massive bull. As hunting weapons, the bow and arrow were superior to the single-shot rifle for short-range work from horseback, and were not supplanted until the introduction of repeating firearms in the nineteenth century.

Catlin exercised a certain amount of artistic license to add excitement to his portrayals of the buffalo chase. He liked to show horse and rider going after big bulls in spectacular close combat. In actual fact, the Indians usually killed cows and calves, whose thinner hides and more palatable flesh were much preferred to those of tough and stringy bulls.

the approach of the hunters for a final death stroke. Several of the wounded cows charge furiously, and only adept maneuvering averts the goring of a horse. Calves of the year are killed easily as they linger by their dams. Soon the butchering begins, and boys bring up riderless horses to carry the meat and hides.

Back at camp the parties come in. There will be no shortage this night. Fires burn brightly, and the feasting and dancing continue until dawn.

This was something different from that hunt of earlier times, which we saw at the Montana buffalo jump. The new plains Indian has vastly improved methods. He runs the herds down in open chase, and his weapons are well suited to this hunter's life. Big hunts still are held in the fall, when supplies are laid in for winter. Sometimes large bands of buffalo can be encircled by horsemen in a "surround" and killed to the last animal. The buffalo jumps still are in use, and so are the long-established pounds into which bands of animals may be driven.

The horse-culture Indians live in spacious skin lodges and commonly have a food surplus. They move easily over their extensive ranges to the constantly renewed pastures

This Catlin painting shows a Sioux encampment on the upper Missouri. Squaws are dressing buffalo robes; beside the tepees, strips of buffalo meat dry in the sun. Virtually every part of the buffalo was useful to the Indians: the dried droppings provided fuel, shoulder blades became hoes, sinews strung bows, horns yielded cups and containers, the ribs were worked into arrowheads—and the tail made an excellent fly swatter!

that feed their working animals and their wild livestock.

In many ways, the horse culture is a fuller and better life. It has brought the plains people more leisure for such pastimes as gambling, art, horse stealing, ceremonial pageantry, and the warfare a man must engage in to gain honor among his people. As men grow in number, some achieve power and influence, becoming rich in horses, squaws, and property. Big nations with many warriors have large hunting claims, which they defend and from which their young men sally forth to surprise, destroy, and rob the enemy.

In less than a century, man has become more significant in the community of the high plains. In many respects his position is more like that of the wolf. For every person there are hundreds of buffalo and many square miles of grass. The diet of the true "horse Indian" is now predominantly meat. He has given up agriculture, although wild food plants still are gathered. Probably the Indian could live well in this vast range for as long as conditions are not changed. He is not damaging his environment or his great food resource, and through wars with his neighbors he limits his own population.

Karl Bodmer, a contemporary of George Catlin, painted this buffalo dance of the Mandan tribe, who, like the Sioux, took up the use of the horse to pursue the buffalo. Unlike the wandering Sioux, however, they were essentially village Indians and practiced agriculture. The presence of guns here indicates direct contact with the white man.

191

The effect of these men on age-old adjustments of the grassland is small, but their relationship to the bison does have a significant difference from that of the wolf. Man is now a highly selective killer in much of his hunting. And he does not "weed out" the poorest buffalo, the weak, diseased, and overaged. He takes the age group that would be most nearly secure from "natural" predation losses, the young, fat, and productive cows. Thus the red man brings another new and strange influence into the wild community that supports him. Others are to follow, as we shall see.

Iron horses, guns, and commerce

Again we must turn the clock of centuries forward. Now we are in the 1870s, and much has happened in a hundred years. European man has multiplied and explored the continent to the Pacific Ocean. Great wagon trails were worn across the plains in the forties and fifties, and in the next decade the railway split the grassland to the Rocky Mountains.

The Indians saw their territory invaded and taken over. Many of them resisted and now are in a running conflict with white soldiers. It is the last war of these open lands. Long ago, buffalo disappeared east of the Mississippi. Remaining herds of the midgrass and shortgrass country westward are under heavy onslaught.

Another revolution in transportation has made this possible. The iron horse of the railway hauls men and supplies westward and takes laden cars of hides back to eastern markets. Now a change in destiny is clear: the prairies and plains are to be farm and ranch country, and the whole world of grass must be made over in a new pattern. The old food linkage is being destroyed. The buffalo is the resource of the warring Indians, and therefore the white man has decided that both must go.

Behind the military front, hide hunters are about their work. As we follow the Atchison, Topeka, and Santa Fe

Stretching from Independence, Missouri, to what is now New Mexico, the Santa Fe Trail poured an ever-increasing flood of white settlers into the West during the middle decades of the nineteenth century.

193

tracks across Kansas, we come to small way stations where great fields of baled hides await shipment.

The last era of buffalo hunting is on. Everywhere in open country, the outfits follow the herds, staying along watercourses where the animals must come to drink. The hunters kill methodically from ambush, commonly at distances of three hundred to four hundred yards. They use breech-loading rifles and load their shells by firelight. Skinners may be at their backbreaking labor from dawn to nightfall, yet many carcasses are left to spoil. Buyers and freighters urge on their multiple teams of mules, dragging heavy wagons for days and weeks across rough lands to the railheads.

By all means, we must visit this camp where a cookfire burns behind a chuck wagon in the early light of dawn. Other wagons stand about on the flat beside the creek. Saddled horses wait as four men finish breakfast and gather their gear. One of them obviously is a hunter, for he carries his rifle and loaded saddlebags as he rides away from the camp. Let us follow him, since this is to be a great day in his career as a buffalo hunter.

As the light grows stronger and our rider is several miles from camp, we see that he is surveying the plain ahead with a field glass. Then he does as thousands of grassland hunters have done before him: he follows the washes in an approach to a high pasture where half a thousand animals are standing about or lying quietly, chewing their cuds. The man in greasy buckskins dismounts beneath a bank and crawls cautiously upward over the edge. Most of the buffalo are about three hundred yards away.

The hunter sets up his three-pronged rest sticks and lays the barrel of his "big fifty" Sharps buffalo gun across them. He sights through a long telescopic sight and then studies the animals carefully with the naked eye. The light is almost good enough for shooting. He opens the breech and slides in a shell from the cartridge belt beside him.

Back in camp the cook and skinner hear the first boom of the big fifty. A few minutes later there is another, then five more at intervals of a few seconds to several minutes. The men stop their work and listen.

"Sounds like Clancy has got himself a stand," says one. "If this keeps up, he'll need another gun and more shells. Think I'll take a sashay out that way."

Clancy does indeed have a "stand," and it will be a long-remembered event. Usually, from a vantage point with his

In the heyday of the professional buffalo hunter, the standard tool of the trade was the Sharps rifle, a hefty weapon that was available in various calibers from .40 to .50 at a cost of $100 to $125. With telescopic sights and carefully hand-loaded ammunition, the Sharps was effective at ranges of up to a hundred yards.

194

long-range weapon, he can kill from one to half a dozen animals before the herd dashes out of range. This morning he has encountered an unusual, but well-known, kind of behavior. The buffalo pay little attention to the shots. A few gather around, smell the blood, and even hook or trample the fallen. The hunter carefully picks animals on the outskirts, and especially alert individuals (commonly cows) who seem about to bolt. Most of the herd stand or lie stupidly and wait.

As black smoke puffs again from the gun, a bull humps his back, walks forward a few steps, and falls over on his side. The skinner, with another gun and a bag of shells, crawls forward to join the marksman. The big fifty is hot, and there is danger of overexpansion of the barrel. With the new weapon the hunter goes to work again. Several hours later, when finally a misplaced shot sends a cow dashing through the herd, the animals scatter, leaving sixty dead on the grass.

The hunter rises stiffly from his labors. He is soaked with sweat, and his hands tremble with fatigue as he lifts the canteen to his lips.

"Still hunting," here portrayed by painter James Henry Moser, was developed into a fine art by the professional buffalo hunters. Through expert marksmanship and careful selection of targets, a good still hunter could sometimes establish a "stand" and drop a hundred or more animals before the herd became alarmed and fled.

195

Clancy and others like him have developed a new kind of mass killing. But now, all but the hides goes to waste. Thousands of hunters with modern guns are killing, not what they must have for food, clothing, and shelter, but as many as they can for the limitless demands of commerce.

The grassland ecosystem has been invaded by a new kind of creature—one so successful that he destroys it. The last of the great buffalo herds will disappear in the early eighties. Trainloads of bones will be hauled away to be ground into high-phosphorus fertilizer. From now on, some of the old annual production of nutrients will not enrich the grassland soil.

The buffalo was the link between grass and Indian. With his living resource gone, the plains Indian can no longer resist the well-equipped soldiers of a higher culture. The red men are at last rounded up and placed on reservations. The vast grassland is open to another stage in its history.

Did we save the buffalo?

Now we must abandon the fantasy of our travels through history. We must come up to modern times and consider the region that was grass and the living things that used it.

We need not follow the Indian further, because he is adopting modern ways. He is no longer a primitive man or necessarily different from anyone else. His chief dependence of centuries past, the buffalo, now is on "reservations" too. The white man needed, and took, the land where grass had fed the wild community.

After the great slaughter of plains buffalo, it appeared that the last of them might be wiped out. But a few wild bison remained in the Yellowstone region, which became a national park, and descendants of those few original animals still are found there. Other buffalo were domesticated (to some extent, anyway) and kept in zoos or private herds. From these some were taken to stock larger ranges in parks and refuges in the grasslands. On such public lands our buffalo has found retreat and is being preserved today—or is it?

We noted that the hunter did something different to the wild herds of horse-culture days: he selected the vigorous young and the cows—something that did not occur in primitive times. The wolf was much more the "undertaker" of a herd, in feeding on overaged and ailing animals. Because

A tragicomic exile for the animal that was once the undisputed monarch of the vast western grasslands: a buffalo is made to play the buffoon for the amusement of a rodeo crowd.

196

the wolf killed as he did, the grass of the plains went to nurture the best of the buffalo. This increased the productivity of the herd and the ecosystem.

Today the white man's buffalo is a beast of quiet pastures where there is no predation at all. To prevent overgrazing of the range, the herds are reduced each year by the killing and butchering of a proper number. How is this done?

Usually some of every age group are taken, to keep a varied and representative herd. But even if he wished, man could not select buffalo for removal as it was done for eons past, by the wolf method that helped make the bison the great beast he is. Today's animal is continuing to change, as nearly all species are, and what it will be like after several centuries of "civilization" is anybody's guess. But it is not likely to be the same buffalo those Indians ran over the cliff in Montana.

Not, that is, unless something comes about which modern biologists frequently discuss. It is the idea of setting aside and restoring a large grassland park, perhaps a million acres, where conditions would be as primitive as possible, where large herds of buffalo would roam and live in an environment much like that of the time before Columbus. Of course, such a park also would be the means of pre-

Deprived of the constant "improvement" exercised by their natural predators, tomorrow's buffalo will not be the same animals that once roamed the plains by the tens of millions.

serving other creatures of the grassland which have not fitted well in the modern pattern.

We could learn from that primitive community of plants and animals how the grassland adapted flexibly to climatic change, how it stored fertility, and how intricate checks and balances operated to keep it going. The area would be a wilderness where man's influence would be kept to a minimum.

Possibly this might be done, for we have only a few small examples of the early prairie and plains ecosystems, and none where the large animals can be truly wild.

Grass for the future

What has happened to the world of grass? Those prairies have become the most productive grain lands on earth. Westward much of the plains country grows dry-farmed wheat. It is a successful operation where soils are right, particularly when a moist climatic phase is on.

In time of drought we get into trouble, for we have broken the sod far beyond the best land and into areas where dry winds pick up great quantities of soil and carry

it eastward in destructive dust storms. In recent years several hundred thousand acres of plowed-up lands have been returned to grass, and it seems likely that this trend will continue under government encouragement. More of the shortgrass and midgrass regions will go back to pasture, added to existing areas where light or rocky soils have been kept in turf since buffalo times, and where cattle take the place of the wild herds that once lived there.

This restoration of grass is encouraging, but it is not taking place everywhere. Some of the remaining northern prairies are being broken for more intensive use under the stimulus of high grain prices. In many areas we can see the marks of implements running up and down the hills instead of on the contour, which would be less damaging. Deltas of fresh topsoil wash into potholes or roadside ditches. This land use will not last forever; the productive period is likely to be short.

Our grasslands have changed since early times. Certainly, for our own well-being, we need to manage them well. Understanding their colorful past—how they served man and beast, how they became rich and productive—should be a good start in guarding them and assuring their benefits to men of the future.

Today the grassland is vastly changed by man-dominated vistas that include buildings, power lines, and windmills. Only the hills and flats, the sun and sky are the same.

Appendix

Grassland Areas Administered by the Department of the Interior

The bulk of North America's great central grasslands are gone past recall. The plow has broken the deep prairie sod and turned its store of riches to the production of corn and wheat; domestic sheep and cattle now graze the range where the great bison and pronghorn herds held sway. Cities linked by railroads and highways now cluster on the Great Plains, and only the place names are left to remind us that this was once red man's country.

Yet it is still possible to step into the past for a little while, to turn the clock back four centuries and experience some of the original grandeur of the prairies and plains that so awed the early white visitors to the American heartland. This is made possible by the work of the United States Department of the Interior, which for more than half a century has been devoted to protecting and perpetuating America's scenic and wildlife legacy.

Several of our national parks and monuments, which are operated by the National Park Service of the Department of the Interior, include regions in which we can observe the American grasslands much as they appeared before the coming of the white man. Less widely known but equally important is the system of national wildlife refuges, administered by the department's Fish and Wildlife Service.

The parks and monuments are intended primarily for the interests of people, so far as these are consistent with the maintenance of these areas in their natural, unspoiled state. The wildlife refuges, on the other hand, are what their name implies—preserves set aside to allow our native birds and animals to escape from the pressure of human competition, and to carry on their life business in undisturbed surroundings. Most refuges are open to the public, however, and some offer limited recreational facilities. Detailed information on any refuge can be obtained by writing to the Director of the Bureau of Sport Fisheries and Wildlife, Washington, D.C. 10240.

Thus, it is still possible to watch bison herds wandering through rolling shortgrass country, to thrill at the sight of ten thousand waterfowl rising from a wet lowland meadow, to laugh at the antics in a bustling town of prairie dogs. The parks, monuments, and wildlife refuges described here belong to you: it is hoped that you will use them and enjoy them.

HAIRY GRAMA

203

SWAINSON'S HAWK

Arrowwood National Wildlife Refuge (North Dakota)
A tract of more than eleven thousand acres of grassland surrounded by the farms of the James River Valley is the major attraction of this refuge, located on Highway 9 near Edmunds, North Dakota. Grazing is permitted on most of the land, and the dominant plants in the grazed areas are smooth brome and Kentucky bluegrass. Scattered throughout the refuge are about six hundred acres of original prairie where big bluestem, switch grass, needle and thread, and green needlegrass can be seen. Among the animals in the refuge are large numbers of migratory waterfowl, white-tailed deer, red foxes, and prairie grouse. Arrowwood is closed during the hunting season; check with the refuge manager before your visit.

Badlands National Monument (South Dakota)
Grasslands alternate with ruggedly eroded hills here, and mixed prairie has largely replaced the original shortgrass plain. Blue grama and needle and thread dominate the higher ground; little bluestem, western wheatgrass, and buffalo grass, the lower. Bison are present but wary, and therefore they are not often seen from the roads. Prairie dogs inhabit a town along an improved road open to visitors. Prairie falcons, sharp-tailed grouse, pronghorns, thirteen-lined ground squirrels, and other wildlife are plentiful. A band of Rocky Mountain bighorn sheep recently transplanted into the monument will give you an idea of what their near relative, the now extinct badlands bighorn, looked like when it roamed this area. See pages 44 and 45.

Benton Lake National Wildlife Refuge (Montana)
Original mixed prairie of green needlegrass, western wheatgrass, and blue grama constitutes half of this 1250-acre wildlife refuge located fourteen miles north of Great Falls, Montana. Benton Lake is a good place to see the rough-legged hawk, Swainson's hawk, sharp-tailed grouse, and burrowing owl, plus a variety of waterfowl. Mammals are represented here by the pronghorn, badger, coyote, jack rabbit, and cottontail. The refuge is open all year, but a federal entrance permit or a daily user permit is required from Memorial Day through Labor Day.

Big Bend National Park (Texas)
This sprawling, rugged park, located in the crook of the Rio Grande's giant U turn, includes approximately a thousand square miles of arid southwestern grassland where sprangletop, tobosa, and black grama flourish. In thickets of mesquite and live oak, you may see white-tailed deer, collared peccaries, coyotes, ringtails, kit foxes, and an occasional cougar. The park's bird life—over two hundred species—is particularly interesting, for it includes many types that are not found farther north. Big Bend is

204

open all year; park officials report that the grass stands are best during the late summer and early fall.

Bowdoin National Wildlife Refuge (Montana)

From U.S. Highway 2, on the border of this refuge seven miles east of Malta in northeastern Montana, you can usually see a herd of pronghorns numbering some 125 animals. About seven thousand acres of original grassland are located here, and grasses of both the shortgrass plains and mixed prairie abound. Western wheatgrass and needle and thread are by far the most common, but blue grama, green needlegrass, and bluebunch wheatgrass are also present. A marsh of some five thousand acres is heavily populated with water birds, including coots, eared grebes, eight thousand ducks of twelve different species, rails, willets, and marbled godwits. In the center of Bowdoin Lake are several small islands on which white pelicans, cormorants, gulls, and great blue herons nest. Many upland birds nest in a six-hundred-acre plot which has been planted with trees and shrubs. The best time to visit Bowdoin is from May through September. Visitors are not encouraged to come during the waterfowl season because of conflict with the hunters.

Carlsbad Caverns National Park (New Mexico)

In addition to the spectacular system of caves that gives it its name, this park includes over seventeen thousand acres of shrub savannah, the distinctive grassland habitat of the southern limit of the American plains. The dominant grasses here are black grama, mountain and burleyleaf muhly, side-oats grama, and tobosa; less common are three-awn grass and hairy grama. The native wildlife includes the mule deer, kangaroo rat, pocket gopher, ringtail, gray fox, and Mexican free-tailed bat. Among the birds, the brown towhee, canyon wren, turkey vulture, scaled quail, and western mockingbird are all common. The park is open all year.

Charles M. Russell National Wildlife Range (Montana)

Since its establishment in 1936, Charles M. Russell National Wildlife Range has been one of the nation's largest federal wildlife management units. This unique wildlife range covers 1,075,411 acres in six counties of north-central and northeastern Montana. It extends upstream on the Missouri River 126 air miles from Fort Peck Dam and varies in width from two to eight miles. Among the grasses in this bunch-grass grassland are western wheatgrass, plains muhly, blue grama, June grass, bluebunch wheatgrass, little bluestem, green needlegrass, and needle and thread. Some 97,021 acres are grassland alone, and 352,336 acres are brush and grassland combined. Along the Missouri River itself there are about 7000 acres of deciduous shrub and cotton-

GREEN NEEDLEGRASS

wood-willow flood-plain forests. Here white-tailed deer are numerous. The badlands, or "breaks," area is the most important big-game habitat for elk, mule deer, and bighorn sheep. The badlands bighorn once roamed here but became extinct about 1923. The plains grizzly and plains wolf have also become extinct. Birds of 193 species have been recorded at the range, among them white pelicans, California and ring-billed gulls, large numbers of double-crested cormorants, and great blue herons. You may visit the range at any time.

Charles Sheldon Antelope Range, Sheldon National Antelope Refuge, and Hart Mountain National Antelope Refuge *(Nevada, Oregon)*

Charles Sheldon Antelope Range and Sheldon National Antelope Refuge, located in extreme northwestern Nevada on the Nevada–Oregon border, and Hart Mountain National Antelope Refuge, near Blitzen in southeastern Oregon, are bunch-grass grassland interspersed with sagebrush. Several species of bluegrass, squirrel-tail, western and bluebunch wheatgrass, Idaho fescue, and Thurber needlegrass grow here. As their names indicate, the primary attraction of these refuges is their herds of pronghorns. The wildlife of the isolated area also includes bighorn sheep, mule deer, sage grouse, and a variety of waterfowl. You can visit here year-round, but a free use permit is required if you want to leave the public roads.

BIGHORN SHEEP

Crescent Lake National Wildlife Refuge *(Nebraska)*

All but 2000 acres of this 46,000-acre tract thirty miles north of Oshkosh is grassland—tallgrass prairie dominated by sand reed grass, sand bluestem, needle and thread, blue grama, sand dropseed, big bluestem, switch grass, Indian grass, and others. On the lake itself is a resident flock of Canada geese, and eighteen species of ducks visit here. Located in the Nebraska sand hills, the refuge has a high water table and many natural lakes on which water birds—especially the waders—thrive. You can always see white-tailed and mule deer here, and at night pocket gophers and kangaroo rats can be observed. The best time to visit is June through August.

Des Lacs National Wildlife Refuge *(North Dakota)*

The Des Lacs Refuge is part of the Souris Loop, which includes the Upper and Lower Souris Wildlife Refuges in north-central North Dakota. The refuge includes nearly ten thousand acres of midgrasses and tallgrasses, with needle and thread, green needlegrass, and western wheatgrass dominant. Located near the dividing line between eastern and western birds, the refuge is a well-known "birding" area, and no less than 259 species have been sighted within its borders. Sharp-tailed grouse are abundant here, as are innumerable waterfowl. Portions of the refuge set aside as recreational areas are open from May 1 to September 30. Other areas may be visited Mondays through Fridays during the spring, summer, and fall when trails are satisfactory for travel. Contact the refuge office for permits and directions.

Fort Niobrara National Wildlife Refuge (Nebraska)
This wildlife refuge was established in 1912 from an old military reservation. Bison and elk were introduced in 1913 and now number three hundred head and forty head, respectively; Texas longhorn cattle, introduced in 1936, have increased to two hundred fifty head. Mixed prairie of midgrasses and tallgrasses makes up sixty percent of the refuge's seventeen thousand acres, the balance being mixed midgrasses and shortgrasses. Fort Niobrara is open throughout the year.

TEXAS LONGHORN

Hutton Lake National Wildlife Refuge (Wyoming)
Western wheatgrass, blue grama, and salt grass dominate the twelve hundred acres of shortgrass prairie encompassed by this refuge near Laramie. The refuge is located on the central flyway, and migratory waterfowl are abundant in the man-made lakes provided for their breeding. Pronghorns, prairie dogs, and Richardson's ground squirrels can be found here. The refuge is open to the public except during the waterfowl season and the midwinter months; at these times it can be visited upon request to the refuge manager.

Kern–Pixley National Wildlife Refuge (California)
Located in the southern part of California's San Joaquin Valley, this refuge will give you a chance to see many of the birds described in this book, for its hundred-odd species include snow geese, a half-dozen different hawks, golden eagles, killdeers, several plovers, marbled godwits, Wilson's phalaropes, and yellow-headed blackbirds. Each year, between mid-August and mid-September, up to a half-million pintail ducks arrive at the refuge. Many grassland mammals make their home here, too—jack rabbits, cottontails, ground squirrels, pocket gophers, various mice, coyotes, kit foxes, badgers, and skunks. The native grasses, which cover twelve thousand acres, are at their best in February and March. The refuge is open all year.

Lacreek National Wildlife Refuge (South Dakota)
Located on the Pine Ridge Sioux Reservation in southwestern South Dakota, the Lacreek Refuge offers four thousand acres of mixed grasses, with salt grass, western wheatgrass, and prairie cordgrass dominant. Birds are a principal attraction; refuge personnel have recorded over two hundred species since 1936, and with luck you may even see the exceedingly rare trumpeter swan.

Both the eastern and western meadowlark are found here, and so avid bird watchers have a chance to compare their songs—the only positive way these birds can be distinguished in the field. Visitors to the refuge are restricted to the trails and roads that the refuge manager has designated as open to the public. Visit any time of the year.

Lostwood National Wildlife Refuge (North Dakota)

There are 22,500 acres of upland prairie at Lostwood. This is shortgrass and midgrass prairie land where green needlegrass and needle and thread are dominant, but areas of crested wheatgrass, little bluestem, switch grass, and western wheatgrass can also be found. The upland prairie comprises about seventy to eighty percent of the refuge, with a 4250-acre underwater area. In wet years the waterfowl production here is very high. Mallards, baldpates, pintails, blue-winged teals, shovelers, redheads, ringnecks, and other ducks are common. There is a large population of white-tailed deer here also. Try a visit in late summer, after the waterfowl nesting season is over, and keep an eye open for sharp-tailed grouse.

PINTAIL

Lower Souris National Wildlife Refuge (North Dakota)

Needle and thread is most abundant in the more than 32,000 acres of grassland here. There is also a wide range of tallgrasses, midgrasses, and shortgrasses. Half of the mixed prairie is original but is scattered through the refuge. Keep a sharp eye out for coyotes, prairie harvest mice, meadow voles, and, among the birds, western meadowlarks, lark buntings, and red-winged and yellow-headed blackbirds. There is a scenic trail running through the sand hills, and trail guides are furnished at refuge headquarters. In addition to the twelve public fishing areas and seven public hunting areas, other areas are open for a late grouse and partridge hunting season. Visit the refuge for bird watching, picnicking, and sightseeing from June 1 to September 30.

Medicine Lake National Wildlife Refuge (Montana)

Medicine Lake is located in extreme northeastern Montana just thirty miles from the Canadian border. The rolling plains here were heavily glaciated during the great ice age, and lakes and potholes dot the reserve. Medicine Lake itself covers 8700 acres. There are some 17,259 acres of prairie here, and midgrasses predominate; the most common species are needle and thread, sand reed grass, western wheatgrass, sand bluestem, alkali grass, and crested wheatgrass. Waterfowl and many other species are abundant here; 204 bird species have been observed since 1935, and nearly a hundred of these nest in or near the refuge. Among the mammals the following are commonly seen by visitors: pronghorns, white-tailed deer, muskrats, red foxes, striped skunks, and

208

white-tailed jack rabbits. One of the most interesting features of Medicine Lake National Wildlife Refuge is its rookery of white pelicans, one of the largest in the United States. The refuge is open from May 1 through December 1 and at other times if the roads are open.

Modoc National Wildlife Refuge (California)
Smooth brome, reed canary grass, timothy, wild rye, and salt grass are the dominant species in the 4200 acres of grassland in this refuge. Nearly half of the grassland is in original condition. Among the animal species are mallards, pintails, cinnamon teals, and large numbers of California quail and ring-necked pheasants. Mule deer and pronghorns are also abundant. Modoc is a natural nesting area for Canada geese. Visit any time; the refuge is near Alturas, California.

National Bison Range (Montana)
This preserve is located in the Flathead Valley some fifty miles north of Missoula. It was established in 1908 primarily for the protection and maintenance of a representative herd of bison numbering about five hundred head. Bluebunch and western wheatgrass, Idaho fescue, Kentucky bluegrass, and rough fescue are the dominant species of grasses here. About 15,679 acres are grassland, and 7055 of these are considered to be in climax condition. The most common mammals and birds are the bison, mule deer, white-tailed deer, pronghorn, Rocky Mountain bighorn sheep, elk, mallard, common goldeneye, Canada goose, marsh hawk, golden eagle, sparrow hawk, blue grouse, gray partridge, killdeer, mourning dove, Wilson's phalarope, and great horned owl. A nineteen-mile self-guiding scenic tour route permits access to virtually all types of vegetation in the refuge, including areas where snowberry, chokecherry, serviceberry, and other shrubs can be seen, and areas of coniferous and broadleaf trees. The wild flowers here are spectacular in spring and early summer. Visit from June 15 until Labor Day. The tour route is open from 8 A.M. until 3 P.M., and the exit gate closes at 5 P.M. Tour participants must remain in or near their cars at all times.

CHOKECHERRY

National Elk Refuge (Wyoming)
Much of this refuge has shortgrass prairie vegetation of the bunchgrass type nestled between the spectacular peaks of the rugged Grand Tetons. Western wheatgrass, Idaho fescue, green needlegrass, and other shortgrasses each year attract thousands of elk, which migrate down from the high country to spend the winter foraging on these and other grass species. A representative exhibition herd of elk is on view from the highway near the refuge headquarters. Another exciting species here is the trumpeter swan. In 1938 some of these swans were transplanted from Red

209

Rock Lakes National Wildlife Refuge, Montana, and in 1944 the first cygnet was raised by a nesting pair. In 1960, seventy-one of these birds were seen in the refuge. Northern portions of the preserve are closed at all times to the public. General regulations of the refuge are available at the headquarters.

Snake Creek National Wildlife Refuge (North Dakota)

This is the only refuge in North Dakota where the pronghorn herds are abundant enough for hunting to be permitted during a limited season. Native shortgrass tracts, ranging in size from a fraction of an acre to about 160 acres, are interspersed with large areas of water throughout the refuge. About one thousand of the seven thousand acres are original grassland, and the dominant plants are green needlegrass, crested wheatgrass, and blue grama. Thirteen-lined ground squirrels, striped skunks, western meadowlarks, mallards, and upland plovers are abundant species. The unusual distribution of water, islands, bays, and peninsulas supports a wide variety of plant and animal life. Snake Creek is located near the town of Coleharbor, in McLean County, central North Dakota. You may visit any time, but the refuge manager prefers that a prior arrangement be made with him.

Theodore Roosevelt National Memorial Park (North Dakota)

Fifty thousand acres of grasslands in the park are reverting to their original condition after an early history of farming and overgrazing. Blue grama is dominant, but little bluestem, buffalo grass, side-oats grama, western wheatgrass, and needle and thread grow here, too. Bison have been reintroduced in the park, and the herd now numbers nearly two hundred head. Prairie dogs are fairly common, as are bobcats. Among the birds, golden eagles and sharp-tailed grouse are numerous. The park is located within the badlands and features bizarre rock formations. It is open all year, and during the summer season park naturalists conduct evening programs in the campgrounds.

WESTERN MEADOWLARK

Turnbull National Wildlife Refuge (Washington)

This refuge covers some 17,171 acres of the extensive lava plains of the Columbia Plateau. The headquarters are located about six miles south of Cheney in Spokane County, Washington. More than thirty-five percent of the refuge is original grassland. The plants, including western wheatgrass, Idaho fescue, Nevada and Sandberg bluegrass, and squirreltail, grow in shallow soils with a low water-holding capacity. The soil conditions and lack of water make this refuge a good place to see grasses growing in the bunchgrass pattern. Many songbirds, shore birds, and water birds can be seen at Turnbull. The coot, pied-billed and eared grebes, killdeer, spotted sandpiper, and black tern all breed abundantly here. Raccoons, mink, northern pocket gophers, badgers, coyotes,

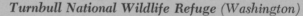

210

mule deer, and white-tailed deer are among the mammals you might see. In order to visit the refuge, contact the manager at headquarters any time of the year.

Union Slough National Wildlife Refuge (Iowa)

More than fifty species of grasses grow in this refuge in north-central Iowa near the Minnesota border. Most conspicuous are those grasses typical of the northern Great Plains and the native grasses characteristic of tallgrass prairie. Pocket gophers, prairie voles, cottontails, meadow jumping mice, western harvest mice, and prairie deer mice are all plentiful.

Upper Souris National Wildlife Refuge (North Dakota)

The headquarters for this refuge are seven miles north of Foxholm, North Dakota. There are nineteen thousand acres of grassland here, but only one thousand acres can be considered to be in original condition. Most of these areas have native grasses such as little bluestem, side-oats grama, switch grass, big bluestem, buffalo grass, June grass, needle and thread, sand dropseed, western wheatgrass, and others common in the shortgrass plains. Much of the native grassland was overgrazed thirty years ago but is not being grazed at present. There is an extensive program of reclamation at Upper Souris: many areas protected from grazing are returning to lush native stands of grass; in other areas native grasses are being planted. The 10,000-acre Lake Darling is a fine spot for fishing. White-fronted geese and whistling swans are here in the fall, and pelicans are about all summer. The most abundant ducks are mallards, gadwalls, and blue-winged teals. The grassland areas in Upper Souris can be visited during spring, summer, and fall.

SAND DROPSEED

Valentine National Wildlife Refuge (Nebraska)

Nearly 60,700 acres of this 72,000-acre refuge are original mixed-grass prairie. There are about a thousand acres of grass that have been ungrazed since 1935 and several other areas where grazing has been abolished from five to ten years. These interesting areas will give you a good idea what the entire region of twelve million acres of unique Nebraska sand hills must have looked like in 1491. Among the grasses growing here are sand bluestem, sand love grass, little bluestem, sandhill muhly, blue grama, and switch grass. You will also see June grass, big bluestem, Indian grass, prairie cordgrass, western wheatgrass, buffalo grass, and others. A live native grass display, with each of the grasses labeled, will help you identify the species. Valentine is primarily a refuge for waterfowl, but sharp-tailed grouse and ring-necked pheasants are common. With luck you might see a greater prairie chicken. To visit Valentine National Wildlife Refuge, travel south of Valentine, Nebraska, on U.S. Highway 83, then thirteen miles west of State Spur 483. Summer or fall is the best time to see the grasses. Visitors are requested to stop at refuge headquarters for information concerning their visit.

Wichita Mountains Wildlife Refuge (Oklahoma)

This refuge is located in the mixed-grass prairies of Comanche County, southwestern Oklahoma. Established as a game preserve by President Theodore Roosevelt in 1905, Wichita Mountains provides a good example of intelligent conservation management in action. In 1907, the buffalo was reintroduced into the refuge when six bulls and nine cows were donated by the New York Zoological Park; today, the refuge's buffalo population stands at nearly a thousand. Similarly, a herd of seventeen elk transplanted from Wyoming has grown to three hundred, and twenty-seven old-fashioned Texas longhorn cattle, introduced in 1927, have increased to three hundred. The refuge also harbors growing herds of pronghorns and white-tailed deer and a prairie-dog town. Over two hundred species of birds have been recorded here, including a population of about three hundred wild turkeys. Of the refuge's sixty thousand acres, nearly half constitute original grassland, with little bluestem, tall bluestem, and hairy grama dominant among the fifty species of grasses recorded. Fifty miles of paved and gravel roads provide access to lakes with swimming beaches, camping and picnic grounds, and other recreational areas.

Wind Cave National Park (South Dakota)

Twenty-three thousand acres of virgin Black Hills grasslands are preserved in Wind Cave National Park, along with much of the original wildlife. Buffalo, elk, pronghorns, and mule deer roam the mixed-grass range, and prairie dogs, badgers, ground squirrels, and other small mammals are common. Virtually every species of grass described in this book can be seen here, along with a wide variety of forbs and wild flowers. Park features include museum exhibits at the visitor center and a self-guiding nature trail that will take you about an hour to cover. The grassland areas of the park are open to the public throughout the year, but park officials feel they are at their best during the autumn.

MULE DEER

Yellowstone National Park (Wyoming, Montana, Idaho)

Yellowstone, the oldest and still the biggest of our national parks, includes among its many attractions some quarter million acres of virgin grasslands, with bunch-grass species predominating. All the major plains animals can be seen in Yellowstone: bison, pronghorns, elk, coyotes, and grizzly bears, plus a wide variety of smaller species. Among the two hundred species of birds recorded in the park are many of the large predatory species and the rare trumpeter swan. Portions of the park are open throughout the year, but the grassland areas, most of which are a mile or more in elevation, are snow-covered during the winter months.

Scientific Classification

A biologist's classification of living things goes further than just "grass" or "gopher." First, he divides them into *kingdoms*: plant or animal. Let us follow the classification of western wheatgrass (*right*) and see how the complete system works. The botanist separates the plant kingdom into a few very large *divisions* on the basis of certain anatomical features (see pages 214 to 217). Grasses, bur oak, gayfeather, to name a few, are placed in the division Spermatophyta (seed plants). However, this division includes so many seed plants that it can be separated into *classes*, one of which, the Angiospermae, or flowering plants, includes western wheatgrass.

Since there are many thousands of flowering plants, classes are broken down into *subclasses*. Plants with a single seed leaf are placed in the subclass Monocotyledoneae. But even this is a huge conglomeration of plants—grasses, conifers, and lilies, for example—and so the scientist divides them again into *orders*. Similarly, orders are divided into *families*, and families into *tribes*. Finally a small group of plants is assigned to a single *genus* (plural *genera*). Although some genera consist of but a single species, most contain several.

Western wheatgrass belongs to the genus *Agropyron*. While there are several species in this genus, ours is the species *smithii*, named in honor of a botanist called Smith.

The strange-looking scientific names of things are really quite simple. They are based on the Latin or Greek languages or latinized forms of other languages. When the system was devised some two hundred years ago, these two languages were the international tongues of scholarship. They have the added advantage of being "dead" languages, no longer spoken: the meanings of their words are not subject to change as are those of "living" languages. No matter where in the world a botanist talks about *Agropyron smithii*, there can be no doubt as to what grass he has in mind.

Common names, on the other hand, often lead to confusion. For example, if you call a grass "June grass" in Indiana, you will probably be understood to mean Kentucky bluegrass, *Poa pratensis*. In Maine, however, June grass is the common name for *Danthonia spicata*, a relative of wild oats usually called poverty oat grass. On the northern prairies, the species called June grass is *Koeleria cristata*, the June grass of this book. Again, the species *Scolochloa festucacea*, which in this book is called whitetop grass, is just as often called sprangletop. No matter how varied the common names for plants and animals are from one locality to the next, their scientific names stay the same.

Kingdom:	Plant
Division:	Spermatophyta (seed plants)
Class:	Angiospermae (flowering plants)
Subclass:	Monocotyledoneae (plants with a single seed leaf)
Order:	Graminales (grasslike plants)
Family:	Gramineae (grasses)
Tribe:	Hordeae (grasses with a single terminal spike)
Genus:	*Agropyron* (wheatgrasses and relatives)
Species:	*smithii* (western wheatgrass)

The Anatomy of a Grass

At first glance, most grasses appear to be very much alike. A closer look, however, shows that these interesting plants have distinctive and clear-cut anatomical features that will help you identify the various species.

Grasses belong to a large subclass of flowering plants called the monocotyledons. You can recognize plants of this subclass by two easily observed features: first, almost all of them have *parallel-veined leaves*; second, all of them have a *single leaf*, or cotyledon, in their seeds. (These so-called seeds are more properly called fruits in all but a few grasses.)

There are only two other kinds of monocotyledons you might confuse with grasses—*sedges* and *rushes*. Sedges usually have solid triangular stems, and their leaf sheaths are not split. Although rushes have round stems like grasses, they are wiry and have many-seeded seed capsules. Grasses, unlike sedges, have round stems that are usually hollow between the nodes, and their leaf sheaths are always split. Unlike rushes, grass stems are not often wiry and—although there are many seeds on a spikelet—always have single seeds between two bracts, a *palea* and a *lemma*.

The major parts of a grass plant are shown at the right. Not all grasses have all the features shown. For example, many grasses do not have stolons; others do not have rhizomes. This generalized grass plant will, however, help you learn the names of the identifying features of the grasses. Some basic clues to grass identification are discussed on the following two pages.

From "Plants From the Grasses" by Richard W. Pohl (Wm. C. Brown Company).

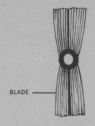

BLADE

CROSS SECTION OF GRASS STEM

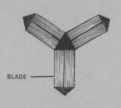

BLADE

CROSS SECTION OF SEDGE STEM

BLADE

CROSS SECTION OF RUSH STEM

PALEA

AWN

SEED

LEMMA

GRASS FRUIT

SEED

BRACT

SEDGE FRUIT

RUSH FRUITS

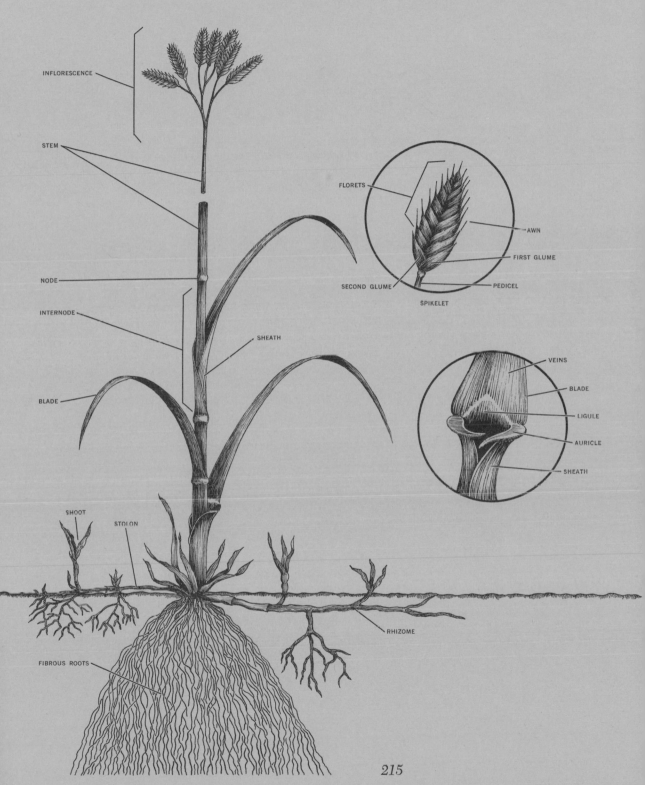

INFLORESCENCE

STEM

NODE

INTERNODE

BLADE

SHEATH

FLORETS

AWN

FIRST GLUME

SECOND GLUME

PEDICEL

SPIKELET

VEINS

BLADE

LIGULE

AURICLE

SHEATH

SHOOT

STOLON

RHIZOME

FIBROUS ROOTS

215

Some Clues for Identifying Grasses

The basic anatomical features illustrated on these two pages will help you understand how grasses are assigned their proper scientific names. In the case of some species, a single outstanding feature is all that is necessary for positive identification. More often, however, identification must be based upon several characteristics, just as a doctor must note several symptoms before accurately diagnosing most diseases.

As a somewhat simplified example, the following features serve to identify a grass plant as western wheatgrass (*Agropyron smithii*):

Inflorescence:	A single terminal, erect spike with many spikelets.
Florets:	Usually six to twelve in each spikelet.
Disarticulation:	Spikelets break off above the glumes.
Rhizomes:	Long, creeping underground stems.
Leaves:	Usually glaucous, or waxy, with a blue color when seen from a distance.
Awns:	The lemmas occasionally have a single stiff "beard."

With a pair of pointed tweezers, a hand lens, and a few other simple tools you can learn to identify most of the grasses growing in your area. You will find two books helpful: *How to Know the Grasses*, by Richard W. Pohl (Wm. C. Brown Company, 1954); and *First Book of Grasses*, by Agnes Chase (Smithsonian Institution, 1959).

Italicized terms on these two pages refer to anatomical features illustrated on page 215.

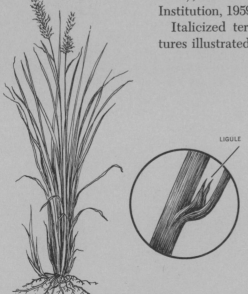

LIGULE

LIGULE. The tonguelike membrane at the base of a grass leaf where the *blade* joins the *sheath* is often a key to the species. The prominent clawlike ligule of Indian grass makes it easy to recognize. In other grasses, such as switch grass, a nest of hair arising from the ligule helps to identify the species. In still others the overlapping of the sheath below the ligule or the shape of the *auricles* may be a clue to identity.

DISARTICULATION. The *spikelets* of grasses often break away from the parent plant when ripe. The location of the break, or disarticulation point, is often important in species identification. In needlegrass and many other species, the break is located above the *glumes*, and the glumes remain on the plant. In other grasses the break is below the glumes, and only the *pedicels* remain.

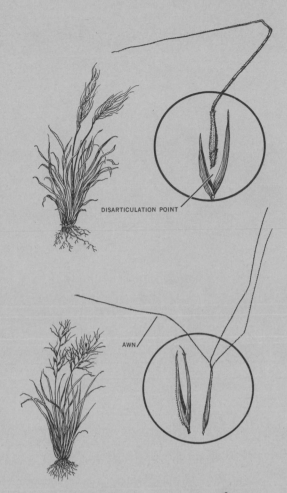

DISARTICULATION POINT

AWNS. The *lemma* of a grass *spikelet* has a midrib that divides it lengthwise, and this rib is often extended into an awn, or beard. Prairie three-awn has a midrib that branches into three awns, a characteristic of a group of species in the genus *Aristida*. The needlegrasses (*Stipa*) have a single awn that may be bent or curled. The presence or absence of an awn is a basic clue to grass classification.

AWN

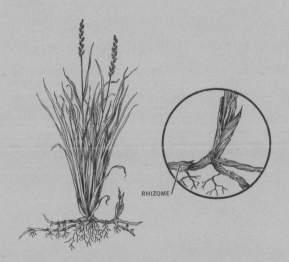

RHIZOME

RHIZOMES. The method of propagation of a grass species is sometimes helpful in identification. Grasses may propagate by seed, by *stolons* (aboveground stems), or by rhizomes (underground stems). Western wheatgrass reproduces from numerous rhizomes as well as by seed. In other grasses propagation may be by rhizomes and stolons, as well as by seeds.

LEAVES. The grass leaf always has *veins* running parallel to each other the length of the *blade*. Side-oats grama has small hairs that project from the edges of the blades, a helpful identifying feature. Prairie cordgrass has a saw-tooth edge. In most grasses the edge is smooth. Often the color of the leaves and its veins are a clue to identification, as are length, width, and other features.

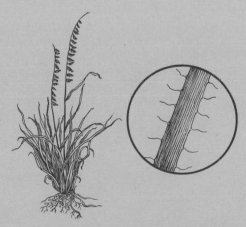

Collecting Grassland Plants

One of the best ways of becoming really familiar with the grasses and forbs of your area is to make a collection of them. The equipment you will need is inexpensive, and the methods used are quite simple. Such a collection will give you a permanent record of your local plant life, ready for your reference and study any time of the year.

Rather than collect plants at random, you might consider selecting a fairly limited area—one particular meadow, say—and concentrating your efforts on it alone. Even a small locality will reveal an astonishing variety of plant life, particularly if you visit at regular intervals throughout the growing season. If you can locate a recently abandoned field or other disturbed site near you, you can build up an interesting collection that shows the succession of vegetation as the site develops into a more permanent grassland type. No doubt other projects will occur to you as you look around the area near your home.

The basic techniques of building a plant collection are shown on these two pages. Your library can supply more detailed information, as well as books to help you identify and study your specimens.

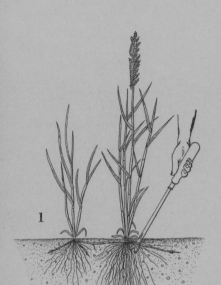

1

1 To dig up the plants you want to add to your collection, you will need a digging tool. A dandelion digger or a large screwdriver will do the job. Work the tool well under the plant, and be sure to get some of the underground parts such as roots and rhizomes, since these may be important for identification of the specimen. Remove dirt from the roots by swishing them in water.

2 Place the plant between a folded sheet of newspaper (tabloid newspapers are ideal). If the plant is too bulky to press flat, divide it carefully and save some of the inflorescences for study

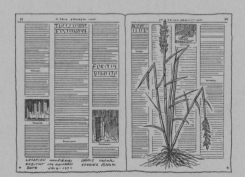

2

later. Bend any long parts. Write the location, habitat, date, and any other pertinent information on the corner of the folded sheet. Grass specimens in their folders can be carried between two sheets of plywood held together by an old belt or a piece of twine.

3 Next the plants must be thoroughly dried. Each plant, still in its folder, should be placed between sheets of deadening felt, which is available at lumberyards. Place a heavy weight on the stacked sheets. Change felts each day, and spread the wet ones in the sun to dry for reuse. The drying process should take about a week.

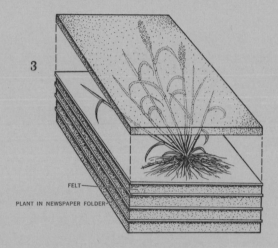

FELT

PLANT IN NEWSPAPER FOLDER

4 Your specimens are now ready for mounting. Special plant-mounting sheets are available from biological supply houses, but Number 6 ledger sheets, from a stationery store, are a good substitute and cost less. Remove the grass plants from their newspaper folders. Arrange each specimen on its own sheet and secure it in place with gummed cloth tape.

Finally, prepare a label listing the information you wrote on the corner of the newspaper and attach it to the lower right-hand corner of the specimen sheet. If you collected extra inflorescences or other parts, they can be placed in a small envelope glued to the sheet. Your plants are now ready for study and identification.

4

Vanishing Animals of the Grasslands

The rich wildlife community of America's great central grassland was the product of tens of millions of years of evolution, yet modern man has undone most of this work of eons in something less than two hundred years. Creature after creature—each a unique and irreplaceable work of nature—has declined before the thrust of civilization. Some have been the victims of heedlessness and greed: the seemingly endless flocks of Eskimo curlews were slaughtered with grim efficiency because there was "sport" or money in it. Others have been exterminated because of real or imaginary threats to the interests of man: the plains wolf and grizzly, the predatory birds, the prairie dogs. Some have declined because we have vastly changed their habitats. In recent years, environmental contamination by chemical pesticides has become a factor in the dwindling of our wildlife resources.

Man is not always to blame when a species dies out. In the natural course of evolution, many living things decline and disappear. But man has often abnormally accelerated this natural process, with violent and far-reaching disruption in the entire wildlife community.

Pictured on these two pages are five representative grassland animals that are teetering on the brink of extinction. Whether they survive or perish depends largely on whether or not we are willing to invest the money and effort needed to save them. That decision must be made today, for tomorrow these creatures will be gone forever.

PRAIRIE FALCON

The prairie falcon is becoming increasingly rare, possibly because of the cumulative effects of pesticide poisons derived from its prey, which may kill the bird outright or render its eggs infertile. Many grassland birds of prey have been severely and often unjustly persecuted by man. The golden eagle, for example, although preying commonly on jack rabbits and other pests, has been heavily hunted by airborne shooters in its wintering grounds in the sheep ranges of Texas.

KIT FOX

This shy little fox with the big ears faces an uncertain future, for it often falls victim to the traps and poisoned baits set out for the larger and more sophisticated coyote. This is unfortunate, for man has no quarrel with the kit fox: the creature lives on kangaroo rats, ground squirrels, grasshoppers, and similar prey. Already extinct in parts of its original range, the kit fox is becoming increasingly scarce throughout the remainder. Even professional conservationists are presently at a loss for ways to reverse this downward trend, although new refinements in predator- and rodent-control research may be helpful.

BLACK-FOOTED FERRET

The black-footed ferret, never very common, has become the rarest of all our mammals with the continued destruction of the prairie-dog colonies on which it depends for both shelter and prey. The ferrets have also been killed by cars or by hunters shooting prairie dogs for sport. Studies are under way in South Dakota to determine if the black-footed ferret can be "transplanted" to the relative safety of prairie-dog colonies within areas of our national parks.

ATTWATER'S PRAIRIE CHICKEN

Of our three remaining subspecies of prairie chickens, Attwater's is in the greatest immediate peril. Formerly distributed over the coastal prairie of Louisiana and Texas, the bird now survives only in small, scattered colonies with a total population of about thirteen hundred. The bird's decline is due not to hunting, against which the law has protected it for many years, but rather to habitat destruction: the tallgrass country it requires is also choice land for grazing and for cultivation of sorghum, rice, and cotton crops.

TULE ELK

The tule elk, smaller and paler than our common elk, has already had one close brush with extinction: it was so heavily hunted for its meat and hide during the California gold rush that its 1885 population dipped to an estimated twenty-eight animals. Intensive conservation efforts have raised the wild population to about four hundred head, now restricted to two California valleys. Local ranchers resent the fact that the animal competes with livestock for available forage and have insisted that its numbers be limited. Perhaps because it so closely resembles the relatively abundant common elk, the tule elk and its plight have received little public interest and support.

Glossary

Adaptation: An inherited characteristic that improves an organism's chances for survival in a particular *habitat*. Adaptations may involve the structure or functioning of an organism's body, as well as inherited behavioral patterns.

Annual: A plant that completes its life cycle from seedling to mature seed-bearing plant during a single growing season, and then dies. *See also* Perennial.

Awn: The beardlike or bristlelike rib protruding from the fruit or seed of some grasses.

Bacteria: Simple, colorless one-celled plants, most of which are unable to manufacture their own food using sunlight. Bacteria are important as *decomposers*.

Biome: A major unit of *habitat*, such as a desert, a spruce-fir forest, or a tallgrass prairie.

Booming ground: The area in which grassland grouse perform their dancelike mating displays.

Browse: To feed on the twigs and leaves of woody plants. Deer and their relatives are browsers. *See also* Graze.

Buffalo chips: Dried buffalo droppings.

Buffalo jump: A site, usually a cliff or steep-sided ravine, which Indians used for mass slaughter of bison by stampeding the animals over a precipice.

Bunch grass: Grasses growing in clusters with bare soil between the groups of plants. This pattern is exhibited primarily by the shortgrasses in the western plains.

Carnivore: An animal that lives by eating the flesh of other animals. *See also* Herbivore.

Carrion: The body of a dead animal.

Cellulose: A carbohydrate found in the cell walls of plants.

Chaparral: Dense scrub vegetation of dwarf trees and thorny *shrubs*.

Chinook: A warm, dry wind that blows down the leeward slopes of the Rocky Mountains.

Chlorophyll: A group of pigments responsible for the green color of plants; essential to *photosynthesis*.

Climate: The average long-term weather conditions of an area, including temperature, rainfall, humidity, wind, and hours of sunlight.

Climax: The relatively stable *community* that represents the end result of *succession* under existing conditions of soil, climate, and other environmental factors.

Community: All the plants and animals in a particular *habitat* that are bound together by *food chains* and other interrelations.

Competition: The struggle between individuals or groups of living things for such common necessities as food or living space.

Conservation: The use of natural resources in a way that assures their continuing availability to future generations; the intelligent use of natural resources.

Consumer: Any living thing that is unable to manufacture food from nonliving substances but depends instead on the energy and nutrients stored in other living things. *See also* Decomposers; Food chain; Primary producers.

Decomposers: Living plants and animals, but chiefly *fungi* and *bacteria*, that live by extracting energy from the decaying tissues of dead plants and animals. In the process, they also release simple chemical compounds stored in the dead bodies and make them available once again for use by green plants.

Drought: A prolonged period when little or no moisture falls on an area.

Ecology: The scientific study of the relationships of living things to one another and to their *environment*. A scientist who studies these relationships is an ecologist.

Ecosystem: A complex system of exchanges of materials and energy between living things and their physical *environment*. The system is repeated in cycles. It is also known as an ecological system.

Entomology: The scientific study of insects. Biologists who specialize in this study are entomologists.

Environment: All the external conditions, such as soil, water, air, and organisms, surrounding a living thing.

Estivation: A prolonged dormant or sleep-like state that enables an animal to escape the rigors of survival during summer months in a hot climate. As in *hibernation*, body processes such as breathing and heartbeat slow down drastically, and the animal neither eats nor drinks.

Evolution: The process of natural consecutive modification in the inherited makeup of living things; the process by which modern plants and animals have arisen through *adaptation* and *natural selection* from more generalized forms that lived in the past.

Food chain: The passage of energy and materials in the form of food from *primary producers* (green plants) through a succession of plant-eating and meat-eating *consumers*. Green plants, plant-eating insects, and an insect-eating animal would form a simple food chain.

Food pyramid: The normally diminishing number of individuals and amount of energy present at each successive level along a *food chain. See also* Trophic levels.

Forage: The plant food of animals, especially those that *graze* or *browse*.

Forb: Any *herb* that is not a *grass* or a *sedge*.

Form: A small protected place, usually a hollow in the grass, where a rabbit or hare rests.

Fossil: Any remains or traces of animals or plants preserved in rock, whether bone, cast, track, imprint, pollen, or any other evidence of their existence.

Fungi (singular *fungus*): A group of plants lacking *chlorophyll*, roots, stems, and leaves. Many fungi are included among the *decomposers.*

Grass: Any plant distinguished by jointed stems, usually (but not always) hollow; two-part leaves consisting of a sheath around a stem and a long, flat blade; tiny flowers borne on small spikes; and dry, seedlike fruit.

Grassland: A vegetation type in which *grasses* are the dominant plants in that they control the energy flow within the ecosystem.

Graze: To feed on grasses. Bison are grazers. *See also* Browse.

Habitat: The immediate surroundings (living place) of a plant or animal.

Herb: Any plant with no permanent parts above the ground, as distinct from *shrubs* and trees.

Herbivore: An animal that eats plants, thus making the energy stored in plants available to *carnivores*.

Hibernation: A prolonged winter dormant period during which an animal's body temperature becomes nearly that of the surrounding environment and its metabolic processes are extremely curtailed. *See also* Estivation.

Humus: Submicroscopic organic particles resulting from the decomposition of dead plants and animals.

Ice age: The epoch, roughly one million to ten thousand years ago, when glaciers covered great parts of the earth.

Incisors: The front teeth of *mammals*, adapted for cutting or gnawing.

Invader: A plant that grows on bare, usually disturbed soil.

Invertebrate: An animal without a backbone. *See also* Vertebrate.

Larva (plural *larvae*): An active immature stage in an animal's life history, during which its form differs from that of the adult. The caterpillar, for example, is the larva of a butterfly. *See also* Nymph.

Legumes: A group of plants many of whose root systems harbor bacteria that convert nitrogen from the air into mineral salts usable by plants.

Lime layer: The stratum of light-colored mineral-rich soil that marks the greatest depth to which rain water penetrates in soils where the rain does not reach down to permanently moist subsoil.

Mammal: Any member of the class of animals that includes bison, rabbits, man, and all other warm-blooded creatures except the birds. Mammals typically have a body covering of hair and give birth to living young, which are nursed on milk from the mother's breast.

Metabolic water: Water produced by all animals as a by-product of digestion, resulting from the recombination of hydrogen and oxygen released in the digestion of sugars. Although the amount of water thus produced is small, some animals, such as kangaroo rats, are so efficient at conserving it that metabolic water is sufficient to maintain proper balance of their body fluids.

Metabolism: The sum of the chemical activities taking place in the cells of a living thing.

Miocene epoch: A geological age about twenty-five to fifteen million years ago.

Mixed prairie: A midgrass and shortgrass zone extending roughly from the Rocky Mountains to Nebraska; a transition belt between the prairie to the east and the plains to the west.

Natural selection: The *evolutionary* process in which forms of living things die off or survive according to their capacity to adapt themselves to the conditions under which they live.

Niche, ecological: An organism's role in a natural *community*, such as seed eater, daytime *predator*, or nighttime predator. The term refers to the organism's function, not the place where it is found.

Nocturnal: Active at night.

Nymph: The immature stage of some insects which closely resembles the adult form except for incompletely developed wings and the inability to carry on reproduction.

Organic: Pertaining to anything that is or ever was alive or produced by a living plant or animal.

Overgrazing: Excessive feeding on the vegetation of an area by wild or domestic animals. Overgrazing results in serious and often lasting damage to the area's ability to support desirable plant life.

Ovipositor: The organ at the tip of the abdomen of female insects, through which eggs are laid.

Panicle: The open, branching flowering parts characteristic of many grasses.

Parasite: A plant or animal that lives in or on another living thing (its host) and obtains part or all of its food from the host's body.

Perennial: Any plant that continues its growth from year to year. In perennial *herbs*, the parts above the ground die away in the fall and are replaced by new shoots in the spring. In the woody perennials, the *shrubs* and trees, permanent woody parts above the ground form the starting point for each year's new growth. *See also* Annual.

Photosynthesis: The process by which green plants unite carbon dioxide and the hydrogen of water into simple sugars. *Chlorophyll* and sunlight are essential to the series of complex chemical reactions involved.

Pothole: A hole, usually circular, carved out by the grinding action of the sand and stones of a glacier.

Prairie: Grassland; an area where the average annual rainfall is usually ten to thirty inches.

Predator: An animal that lives by capturing other animals for food. *See also* Prey.

Prey: A living animal that is captured for food by another animal. *See also* Predator.

Primary consumer: A plant-eating animal; an animal that converts the primary production of plants into animal tissue, thereby making the energy stored in plants available to flesh-eating animals. *See also* Primary producers; Secondary consumer.

Primary producers: Green plants, the basic link in any *food chain*. By means of *photosynthesis*, green plants manufacture the food on which all other living things ultimately depend. *See also* Primary consumer.

Race: A category of individuals within a *species* which differs slightly from the typical members of the species.

Rodent: Any member of a large group of gnawing *mammals*, including rats, mice, squirrels, prairie dogs, and many others. Rodents are characterized by a pair of long, chisellike teeth at the front of both upper and lower jaws, used for gnawing and clipping plant foods.

Ruminant: Any of a group of animals, including cattle, goats, sheep, bison, and deer, whose food is first swallowed partially chewed and later regurgitated as cud to be thoroughly chewed and reswallowed.

Scavenger: An animal that eats the dead remains and wastes of other animals and plants.

Secondary consumer: An animal that feeds on plant eaters. Plants (*primary producers*), plant eaters (*primary consumers*), and *predators* (secondary consumers) would form three links in a *food chain*. *See also* Third-order consumer.

Sedge: A kind of plant resembling the grasses. However, sedges usually have solid triangular stems in contrast to the round hollow stems of grasses.

Shrub: A woody plant, usually less than twelve feet tall and having many stems rising from the ground.

Sod: Thick, tough masses of grass roots growing in the soil of the grasslands.

Soil profile: A section of soil from the surface downward in which the major soil zones, or horizons, may be seen. The three horizons—topsoil, subsoil, and slightly altered parent material—differ in depth and composition depending on the climate, vegetation, topography, and other factors.

Species (singular or plural): A group of plants or animals whose members breed naturally only with each other and resemble each other more closely than they resemble members of any similar group.

Succession: The gradual replacement of one *community* by another, usually leading to a more or less stable *climax* community.

Talus: A sloping pile of rock fallen from a cliff.

Territory: An area defended by an animal against others of the same species. It is used for breeding, feeding, or both.

Third-order consumer: A *predator* that feeds on *secondary consumers*.

Travois (pronounced *travoy*): A dog- or horse-drawn vehicle used by plains Indians for transporting goods. It consists of a platform or net hung between two trailing poles that are attached to each side of the animal.

Trophic levels: Feeding levels in a *food chain*, such as *primary producers, herbivores,* and so on. Most food chains include a maximum of four or five trophic levels.

Vertebrate: An animal with a backbone. The vertebrate group includes fishes, amphibians, reptiles, birds, and *mammals. See also* Invertebrate.

Water table: The upper level of the underground reservoir of water, below which the soil and all cracks and channels in the rocks are saturated. The water level in different areas may lie at the surface or hundreds of feet underground and, depending on rainfall and rate of removal of the water, may fluctuate from time to time in any given area.

GRASSES AND GRASSLANDS

BARNARD, COLIN (Editor). *Grasses and Grasslands*. St Martins, 1964.

CHASE, AGNES. *First Book of Grasses*. Smithsonian Institution, 1959.

POHL, RICHARD W. *How to Know the Grasses*. William C. Brown, 1954.

POOL, RAYMOND J. *Marching with the Grasses*. University of Nebraska Press, 1948.

SPRAGUE, HOWARD B. (Editor). *Grasslands*. American Association for the Advancement of Science, 1959.

U.S. DEPARTMENT OF AGRICULTURE. *Grass: The Yearbook of Agriculture, 1948.* U.S. Government Printing Office, 1948.

WILSON, CHARLES M. *Grass and People*. University of Florida Press, 1962.

ANIMAL LIFE

ALLEN, DURWARD L. *Our Wildlife Legacy*. Funk & Wagnalls, 1962.

BARKER, WILL. *Familiar Insects of America*. Harper & Row, 1960.

BOURLIÈRE, FRANÇOIS. *The Natural History of Mammals*. Knopf, 1964.

BUCHSBAUM, RALPH. *Animals Without Backbones*. University of Chicago Press, 1948.

BUCHSBAUM, RALPH, and LORUS J. MILNE. *The Lower Animals*. Doubleday, 1961.

CAHALANE, VICTOR H. *Mammals of North America*. Macmillan, 1947.

HAMILTON, W. J. *American Mammals*. McGraw-Hill, 1939.

HUTCHINS, ROSS E. *Insects*. Prentice-Hall, 1966.

MATTHIESSEN, PETER. *Wildlife in America*. Viking, 1965.

ROE, FRANK G. *North American Buffalo*. University of Toronto Press, 1951.

SCHWARTZ, CHARLES W. *Prairie Chicken in Missouri*. University of Missouri Press, 1944.

SCHWARTZ, CHARLES W., and ELIZABETH R. SCHWARTZ. *Wild Animals of Missouri*. University of Missouri Press, 1959.

ECOLOGY

ALLEE, W. C., and others. *Principles of Animal Ecology*. Saunders, 1949.

ANDREWARTHA, H. G. *Introduction to the Study of Animal Populations*. University of Chicago Press, 1961.

BENTON, ALLEN H., and WILLIAM E. WERNER, JR. *Principles of Field Biology and Ecology*. McGraw-Hill, 1958.

BUCHSBAUM, RALPH, and MILDRED BUCHSBAUM. *Basic Ecology*. Boxwood Press, 1957.

CLEMENTS, FREDERIC E., and VICTOR E. SHELFORD. *Bio-Ecology*. Wiley, 1939.

DAUBENMIRE, R. F. *Plants and Environment*. Wiley, 1959.

ELTON, CHARLES. *The Ecology of Animals*. Methuen, 1933.

KENDEIGH, S. CHARLES. *Animal Ecology*. Prentice-Hall, 1961.

ODUM, EUGENE P., and HOWARD T. ODUM. *Fundamentals of Ecology*. Saunders, 1959.

OOSTING, HENRY J. *The Study of Plant Communities*. Freeman, 1956.

SHELFORD, VICTOR E. *The Ecology of North America*. University of Illinois Press, 1963.

STORER, JOHN H. *The Web of Life*. Devin-Adair, 1960.

WEAVER, J. E. *North American Prairie*. Johnsen, 1954.

WEAVER, J. E., and F. W. ALBERTSON. *Grasslands of the Great Plains*. Johnsen, 1956.

WEAVER, J. E., and F. E. CLEMENTS. *Plant Ecology*. McGraw-Hill, 1938.

FIELD GUIDES

LUTZ, FRANK E. *Field Book of Insects*. Putnam, 1948.

MURIE, OLAUS. *A Field Guide to Animal Tracks*. Houghton Mifflin, 1954.

PALMER, RALPH S. *The Mammal Guide*. Doubleday, 1954.

PETERSON, ROGER TORY. *A Field Guide to Western Birds*. Houghton Mifflin, 1961.

POUGH, RICHARD H. *Audubon Western Bird Guide*. Doubleday, 1957.

HISTORY

BRANCH, E. DOUGLAS. *Hunting of the Buffalo*. University of Nebraska Press, 1962.

BURROUGHS, RAYMOND DARWIN (Editor). *The Natural History of the Lewis and Clark Expedition*. Michigan State University Press, 1961.

EWERS, JOHN C. *The Blackfeet: Raiders on the Northwestern Plains*. University of Oklahoma Press, 1958.

EWERS, JOHN C. *The Horse in Blackfoot Indian Culture*. Bulletin 159, Bureau of American Ethnology, U.S. Government Printing Office, 1955.

GREGG, JOSIAH. *Commerce of the Prairies*, edited by Archibald Hanna. Lippincott, 1962.

GRINNELL, GEORGE B. *When Buffalo Ran*. University of Oklahoma Press, 1966.

HYDE, GEORGE E. *Indians of the High Plains: From the Prehistoric Period to the Coming of the European*. University of Oklahoma Press, 1959.

KRAENZEL, CARL FREDERICK. *The Great Plains in Transition*. University of Oklahoma Press, 1955.

MACLEOD, WILLIAM C. *The American Indian Frontier*. Knopf, 1928.

MARTIN, PAUL S., GEORGE I. QUIMBY, and DONALD COLLIER. *Indians before Columbus*. University of Chicago Press, 1947.

ROBBINS, ROY M. *Our Landed Heritage: The Public Domain, 1776–1936*. Princeton University Press, 1942.

UNDERHILL, RUTH MURRAY. *Red Man's America*. University of Chicago Press, 1953.

WEBB, WALTER PRESCOTT. *The Great Plains*. Ginn, 1931.

WEDEL, WALDO R. *Prehistoric Man on the Great Plains*. University of Oklahoma Press, 1961.

WISSLER, CLARK. *North American Indians of the Plains*. American Museum of Natural History Handbooks, No. 1, 1934.

Illustration Credits and Acknowledgments

COVER: Trek to water, Durward L. Allen

ENDPAPERS: J. M. Conrader

UNCAPTIONED PHOTOGRAPHS: 8–9: Reed canary grass, Durward L. Allen 58–59: Prairie dog, Durward L. Allen 126–127: Pronghorns, Durward L. Allen 168–169: Albert Bierstadt, "The Last of the Buffalo," in the collection of the Corcoran Gallery of Art

ALL OTHER ILLUSTRATIONS: 10–11: Wilford L. Miller 12: Laurence Lowry 13: Mark Binn; Alfred Gross from National Audubon Society 14–15: Patricia C. Henrichs 16: Gene Hornbeck 16–17: John R. Clawson 18: Graphic Arts International 19–20: Jack Dermid 21: Thase Daniel 22: Grant Heilman 24–25: Hans Zillessen from G.A.I. 26: Mark Binn; J. M. Conrader 27: Durward L. Allen; John R. Clawson 28: Robert W. Mitchell; Durward L. Allen 29: Durward L. Allen 30: Mark Binn; Durward L. Allen 31: Durward L. Allen 32: B. B. Jones 33–34: Durward L. Allen 35: Ed Park 36–37: Durward L. Allen 38: Hans Zillessen from G.A.I. (Skinner and Kysen) 39: Mark Binn 40: Charles Fracé 41: Robert W. Mitchell 42–43: Durward L. Allen 44–45: Roche 46–47: Durward L. Allen 48: Mark Binn 48–50: Robert W. Mitchell 51: Durward L. Allen 52–53: Graphic Arts International 54–70: Durward L. Allen 71: Wilford L. Miller 72: Harry Engels 72–73: Leonard Lee Rue; Durward L. Allen; William W. Dunmire 74: W. J. Schoonmaker 75: Leonard Lee Rue 76–77: Ed Cesar 78: Norman Lightfoot 79: Ed Cesar 80–81: Charles Fracé 82: Walter R. Spofford 83: Robert W. Mitchell 84: Patricia C. Henrichs 85: Verna R. Johnston 86–88: Patricia C. Henrichs 89: Evan J. Davis 90: Durward L. Allen 91: Wilford L. Miller 92: Thase Daniel 95: John Hopkins, National Audubon Society 96: Glenn D. Chambers 97–98: John Hopkins, National Audubon Society 100–103: Ed Cesar 104–105: Wilford L. Miller 106: Robert Strindberg 107: James Kern 108–110: Durward L. Allen 111: Robert Strindberg 112: F. W. Lahrman from National Audubon Society 113: Harry Engels 114: Gerald Swenson 116: Leonard Lee Rue 117: Mark Binn (Audubon magazine) 118–119: John Hopkins, National Audubon Society 120: Walter R. Spofford 121: Ed Park 122: George M. Bradt 123: R. J. Austing from Photo Researchers 124: Durward L. Allen 128–129: Richard Scheich 130: Paul R. Nesbitt 131: Stephen Collins; Robert W. Mitchell 132: Hans Zillessen from G.A.I. (from Zim and Cottam) 133: George M. Bradt 134: Robert W. Mitchell 135: Durward L. Allen; Edward S. Ross 136: Grant Haist 137: Robert W. Mitchell 138: Patricia C. Henrichs 139: Mark Binn 140–141: Hans Zillessen from G.A.I. 142–143: Durward L. Allen 144–145: Robert W. Mitchell 146–148: Charles Fracé 149–151: Robert W. Mitchell 152–153: Wilford L. Miller 154: Gene Hornbeck 156–157: George M. Bradt 158: Leonard Lee Rue 159: Wilford L. Miller from National Audubon Society 160–161: Gerry Atwell 162–163: Smithsonian Institution 164: Hans Zillessen from G.A.I. 166: Durward L. Allen 171: Smithsonian Institution 172: Hans Zillessen from G.A.I. 174–175: John Hopkins (courtesy of Dr. C. Campbell Stiles and by permission of the family and the executors of the estate of Ethel Traphagen Leigh) 177–179: Joe Ben Wheat 180–181: Patricia C. Henrichs 182: Courtesy of the New-York Historical Society, New York City 183: Smithsonian Office of American Ethnology Collection 184–187: Smithsonian Institution 188–189: Courtesy of the New-York Historical Society, New York City 190–191: Smithsonian Institution 192: Peter G. Sanchez 194: Mark Binn 195: Smithsonian Institution 196: Dennis Stock from Magnum 197: Durward L. Allen 198–199: Robert W. Mitchell 201–212: Charles Fracé 214–217: Patricia C. Henrichs 218–219: Mark Binn 220–221: Charles Fracé

PHOTO EDITOR: ROBERT J. WOODWARD

ACKNOWLEDGMENTS: *The author wishes to thank the following individuals for their technical counsel, their identification of specimens, or their helpful participation in his field work: Byron O. Blair, Professor of Agronomy, Purdue University; Alton A. Lindsey, Professor of Biology, Purdue University; Elroy L. Rice, Professor of Botany, University of Oklahoma; Robert F. Betz, Professor of Biology, Illinois Teachers College North; Mrs. J. Wayne Cole, Deerfield, Illinois; Marshall White, Graduate Research Assistant, Purdue University; Floyd A. Swink, Taxonomist, the Mortaon Arboretum; Robert C. Fields, Manager, Fort Niobrara National Wildlife Refuge; John A. Tyers, Chief Naturalist, Wind Cave National Park; Lary D. Barney, Ranger, Theodore Roosevelt National Memorial Park; Robert E. Stewart, Biologist, Northern Prairie Wildlife Research Center; Arthur F. Halloran, Regional Biologist, Bureau of Sport Fisheries and Wildlife; Cordia J. Henry, Manager, National Bison Range.*

The publisher is particularly grateful to F. C. Gillett, Chief, Division of Wildlife Refuges, to C. Gordon Fredine, Chief, Division of International Affairs of the National Park Service, and to the park superintendents and refuge managers who responded in detail to a questionnaire on grassland areas administered by the Department of the Interior. The publisher also wishes to thank the following individuals: William Perry, Neil J. Reid, Douglass Hubbard, and M. Woodbridge Williams of the National Park Service for their assistance in reading the manuscript or locating photographs; Robert W. Lanni for supervising the photographing of paintings in the collection of the Smithsonian Institution, Washington, D.C.

Index